Way Back in the Country Garden

Living off the earth's yield for six generations:
an East Texas farm family's
recipes and stories

Kay Wheeler Moore

HANNIBAL BOOKS
www.hannibalbooks.com

In a bygone day, in a place perhaps not too different from one your family calls home . . .

Mattie faced a giant dilemma involving her youngest daughter, Mable.

Her carrot-topped offspring wanted to wear her new blue silk, Sunday-best dress to the Delta County fair. Mable refused to get dressed in her everyday calico; her antics were detaining her older sisters, Bonnie and Frances, who already were headed for the wagon. Papa had the team saddled up for the six-mile trip into Cooper so the family could attend the long-awaited event.

Mattie was in a hurry, too. She was eager to arrive at the fair to enter her chow-chow in the judging for Best Relish. For the ride into town her bottle of the prized, colorful relish already was wrapped up in paper and tied with string. She feared Mable would tear her dress as she and her siblings moseyed around the fairgrounds with all the activities there, but the fiery-haired youngster could not be persuaded. At that moment Mable, with arms crossed defiantly, stood stubbornly on the stairs.

What was Mattie to do? Give in to her youngest and risk ruining the beautiful dress that Mattie had worked so diligently to stitch for Mable? Continue to cajole the girl and run the risk of missing the relish contest? Stay home with the rebellious child and let the rest of the family go to the fair without their Mama?

The antics of the Three Red-Haired Miller Girls—and the memorable, homespun recipes that their family and descendants prepared—continue . . ..

Published by
Hannibal Books
PO Box 461592
Garland, TX 75046-1592
Copyright Kay Moore 2010
All Rights Reserved
Printed in the United States of America
by Lightning Source, La Vergne, TN
Cover design by Greg Crull and Amy Harvey
Line drawings, page 135, by Malcolm Wilson

All Scripture taken from the Holy Bible,
New International Version, copyright 1973, 1978, 1984
by International Bible Society
ISBN 978-1-934749-71-5
Library of Congress Control Number 2010900915

TO ORDER ADDITIONAL COPIES SEE PAGE 221

Contents

The Town that Is No More   9

Chapter 1
"We Were Rich"   11
    Tomato Preserves   16

Chapter 2
A Fair Amount of Wisdom   17
    County Fair Chow-Chow   23

Chapter 3
Five Women in a House   24
    Baked Stuffed Onions   30

Chapter 4
Downtown   31
    Sauteed Okra, Corn, and Tomatoes   36

Chapter 5
In the Garden Alone   37
    Plum-Peach Crumble   44

Chapter 6
A Cake Never Baked   45
    Strawberry Layer Cake   49

Chapter 7
One Smart Indian   50
    Three Sisters Stew   59

Chapter 8
   A Sweet Taste of Victory   60
      Butter Beans and Ham   68

Chapter 9
   Little Dusty and the Missing Wedding Dress   69
      Pork and Lima Skillet   75

Chapter 10
   Pumpkin Anything   76
      Pumpkin-Pecan Pie   83

Chapter 11
   No Room at the Inn   84
      Cinnamon Apples   91

Chapter 12
   Peach Trees and the Wedding Plywood   92
      Quick Peach Cobbler   103

Chapter 13
   To Love, Honor, and Surprise   104
      Cucumbers and Onions in Vinegar   111

Chapter 14
   Blessed Be the Name of the Lord   112
      Blackberry Cobbler   124

Family Tree   126
Family Album   127
Recipes   135
Index   215

Dedicated

to the memory of

Margaret Frances Miller Oyler
(1907-2009)

The last of the Three Red-Haired Miller Girls—
all now safely Home—together
and with their sweethearts.

Thank you, Aunt Frances,
for 102 years
of stories,
recipes,
and love.

Frances and Herbert as I like
to envision them now—
forever young and in love

Miller home in Brushy Mound (TX)
before house was razed

Note about Health-Conscious Food Preparation:

We urge readers to use every means possible to cook healthy. We implore those who prepare these recipes to tailor them to their specific health needs: use salt substitute, unsalted butter, low-sodium soups and sauces, skim or 1-percent milk, ground turkey instead of ground beef, cooking spray instead of butter or shortening to grease pans, egg substitute instead of whole eggs, sugar substitute when possible, etc. Although recipes in most cases do not feature these substitutions, any recipe contained herein may be adapted to suit the health requirements of the person dining. We want you and your family members to be on this earth for a long, long time and urge you to be kind to your health when you cook!

The Town that Is No More

Let me take you driving to the town
    that is no more.
You'll not see homes nor churches,
    no school nor general store—
Only tall-grown fields of weeds
    where children used to play—
One lone, brush-hidden monument
    to mark a bygone day.

But if you listen carefully—let
    imagination fly—
You'll hear the sounds of little girls
    who lived in times gone by.
Their home was in the country, like
    everyone's back then.
Their papa was a farmer just like
    all the other men.

The empty fields, so lonely now,
    here once were flower-strewn.
Running through them gaily was
    the best play ever known.
So, long before computers and
    games that entertain,
These children made an afternoon
    of splashing in the rain.

Grandma lived just up the road;
    cousins lived next door.
Kinfolk were their playmates; how
    could they want for more?
Their people—poor as churchmice,
    But these children never knew.
Their table flowed with bounteous
    food that from the garden grew.

Their dress was *fashionista* with
    attire not from the store.
Their mom with thread and needle
    over patterns she would pore.
Church on Sundays was a must,
    and in the afternoon
They'd chat with friends and kin-
    folk 'til the rising of the moon.

Those trees that overarch the road,
    they once provided shade
For fellowships and suppers served
    in boxes all handmade.
The outdoor arbors sheltered scenes
    of tent revivals here—
Where gospel tunes poured out
    from hearts so ardent and sincere.

Where is the town that is no more?
    Where did its people go?
Progress lured them far away. The
    townsfolk moved, and though
Their hearts remained in places
    dear, they knew for future's sake
To set aside their rural lives, with
    urban steps to take.

One by one the vacant homes
    went crumbling to the ground.
The stores and churches full of life
    No longer can be found.
And so, unless your heart is
    schooled to see beyond the brush,
You'll miss this site and speed on
    by in this day's frantic rush.

Dear daughter mine, with hair of
    gold, who rides with me today,
Your life is shaped by what was
    here much more than I can say.
The things that are the best of
    you—that form your very core
Had their roots in what you pass—
    the town that is no more!

—KWM

*Guard the good deposit that was entrusted to you—
guard it with the help of the Holy Spirit who lives in us*
(2 Tim. 1:14).

A modern-day Christmas feast at Yvonne's—the tradition
lives on, the long-ago draws near.

Chapter 1
"We Were Rich"

The screen door to the farmhouse creaked open and then quickly slapped shut.

Without glancing up from her ironing board Grandma Harris knew the next sound would be that of feet *pit-patting* from the front porch into the living room and halting abruptly at her dining table.

Those feet, Grandma knew, could belong to any of several of her grandchildren, whose stopovers at her house were part of their regular home-from-school itinerary.

"Oh, *yum*, she's got a fresh bowl full," Grandma heard a high-pitched squeak emerge. That would be Mable, the youngest of Grandma's daughter, Mattie, who lived across the pasture with her family.

"I was here first, Mable," a slightly older voice cajoled. Frances, Grandma's namesake, got irritated easily with her smaller sibling. "Don't hog the crackers so I can have the first dip."

"We've all gotta be quick before the others get here," the oldest one, Bonnie, warned her younger two sisters. They glanced over their shoulders to see whether any of their cousins were hungrily making their way onto Grandma's porch.

"Girls, I got plenty of tomato preserves fer ever'one—for you and yer cousins," Grandma gently chided. She stepped from the kitchen to hug her granddaughters, who competed for the first taste of the thick, sweet treat that awaited them as an afternoon snack. "Take turns, now, so I won't have t' tell yer mama ya didn't share politely."

Grandma Harris had put out the new batch of tomato preserves earlier that day after Grandpa fetched several jars from the storm cellar which had housed them since the summer's canning. Grandma's long, hot days of putting up delightful red tomatoes from their garden had yielded a treasure trove of preserves Grandma could share throughout the fall and winter.

In mid-afternoon Grandma had opened the first jar and ladled its contents into a wide-rimmed, cutglass compote that stood on a gleaming, glass-stemmed pedestal in the center of her dining table. The cutglass glistened like diamonds as it reflected the sun's light filtering through the room. Into a separate dish Grandma had set out some saltine crackers. On this particular afternoon her red-haired granddaughters—Bonnie, Frances, and Mable Miller—were the first snack-seekers.

No doubt they'd soon be followed by some of the youngsters of her other sons and daughters whose homes were also nearby.

Ultimately Grandma Harris would go on to begat 52 grandchildren in all, but she never ran out of treats for them or resourceful ways to prepare the many vegetables that she and Grandpa Harris grew in their everlastingly prolific garden. Every Sunday Grandma prepared an enormous, after-church dinner for all of her 11 children and their families who could attend.

Because their farmhouse was closest to Grandma's, the "Three Red-Haired Miller Girls", as many in their community of Brushy Mound knew them, hardly ever missed a Sunday—or an after-school afternoon—at Grandma's house, where her good cooking always abounded.

* * * * * * * * * *

A century later the Harris farmhouse built on the rich, black soil of Delta County, TX, has long ago crumbled down. Grandma's abundant garden has been plowed under with only a few derelict weeds to mark the spot where those sweet-as-candy tomatoes grew so bountifully. For more than 65 years grass has grown unbidden around the tombstone marked "Frances E. Harris"—the Miller girls' beloved "Grandma".

But down all the decades, the memory of Grandma's delectable tomato preserves served in the sparkling, pedestaled compote would remain fresh in the mind of her namesake—little Frances, who was still recounting the tomato preserves story well into her 103rd year on this earth.

"We were rich," Frances recalled to us nieces and nephews, who discreetly pumped her for *just one more* of her "olden-days" country tales before night would fall on her memory forever. This font of family lore was the last surviving member of that generation of our kin. At 102 years and 1 month of age Frances could still describe picking melons the size of basketballs, okra rows that were city blocks-long, and cornstalks that seemed to stand tall as skyscrapers.

Although farm families such as hers usually lacked financial means, the garden insured that no one would go hungry. Just before supper each night Mama faithfully sent Frances and her sisters out to see what was ready to be plucked from the vine and cooked up for that night's meal.

"We had no idea we were poor," Frances mused from her wheelchair, "because we always had food from the garden."

* * * * * * *

At the time Frances related her last tomato preserves story before her passing in May 2009, people everywhere were turning to backyard patches of earth again for the same reason the Miller girls and their mama and grandma did in the early part of the last century.

Economic woes in the United States and around the world have caused family incomes to plummet. Home-gardening has become a passionate new interest for people who have never planted a seed or worked a hoe. Even the wife of the U.S. President at the time, as an example for others, grew vegetables in her own White House garden. Heads of households can gaze on small stretches of garden dirt and comfort themselves in the same way Frances' family did. After all, the Great Depression, which clouded the Miller Girls' youth in rural northeast Texas, did not sting as much to those who could till the soil and cultivate its yield. With food from the garden, they could always feed their families and feel "rich", no matter how lean the times or how thin the pocketbook.

My earlier cookbook, *Way Back in the Country*, emphasized that food, the recipes for how to prepare it, and the stories of people who cooked them are all interwoven into the fabric of family life. *Way Back in the Country* encouraged families to preserve not just their legendary recipes but the lore of the loved ones—such as the indomitable Grandma Harris—who made them popular. Through tales of the Red-Haired Miller Girls—my mother, Mable, and her two sisters, Frances and Bonnie—and six generations of their farm kin and the recipes that have been regulars at family gatherings for decades, *Way Back in the Country* inspired others to get their tape-recorders out and investigate why "Great-Aunt Gertie" always brought lemon pound cake whenever their extended families dined.

With gardening surging in popularity once more, the time seems right to revisit the Miller-Harris legends and recipe chests—this time to celebrate the role that food from one's own soil has always played in American homes and how, in the Tight Times of this Great Recession, it makes us feel "rich" with hope and comfort afresh. *Way Back in the Country Garden* again will intertwine six generations of my family's anecdotes with cooking instructions that will probably remind you of some of your own family favorites.

So prepare to laugh, cry, and traipse down memory lane once again with the Red-Haired Miller Girls and their progeny—through yarns my family told—yarns that I didn't always witness firsthand but can try to recreate as I can envision them happening in my mind's eye.

May you soon be preserving some country gardening tales of your own and savoring the memories and tastes of yesterday.

Tomato Preserves

7 pounds tomatoes, peeled and cut in chunks
5 pounds sugar
4 lemons, thinly sliced
1/4 cup ground ginger

In a kettle combine tomatoes, sugar, and lemons. Cook slowly until the tomatoes are transparent and begin to thicken; stir in ginger. Cook slowly for 5 minutes; pour into sterilized jars and seal.

Chapter 2

A Fair Amount of Wisdom

The Three Red-Haired Miller Girls were as fidgety as butter pats on a griddle.

Mattie had to practically arm-wrestle Bonnie and her younger sisters, Frances and Mable, to get them to down just *half* their morning bowls of oatmeal. Nobody seemed the faintest bit interested in breakfast.

"Do you think they'll have cotton candy?" Mable, who was 5, queried her sisters. "It's so sweet and fluffy."

"They had gumdrops last year," Frances, 9, recalled. "I like the purple and orange ones best."

Bonnie, a year older than Frances, had other goals in mind. "I hope they have the ring-toss again. I'd love to win a prize." She remembered how their cousin, Jessie Harris, once brought home a crystal dish when she tossed her lucky penny at the arcade.

Papa stuck his head in the door and interrupted. "When'll th' gals be ready, Mattie? I hear 'em junin' around in thar. I'm harnessin' th' team so we can head t' town."

Mattie shooed the three carrot-tops upstairs so they could put on their dresses. Then she took a jar of freshly made chow-chow relish off the shelf and held it up to the light before she began wrapping the container in brown paper.

Thick and colorful, with clear brine, she assessed as she tossed an approving nod to her creation that combined her home-grown cabbage, onion, and red peppers. *I hope th' judges will like it.*

Several layers of paper cushioned the glass jar so it wouldn't break on the wagon ride into Cooper for the Miller family to attend the annual Delta County fair. Then Mattie tied a string around the sides and another around the top of the bundle to fasten the paper securely.

From the stairs trumpeted a wail. "I can, too, wear it, Frances," Mattie heard her youngest bellow. She looked up to see Mable clutching her new, blue-silk frock that Mattie had fashioned her for "Sunday-go-to-meetin'."

"Mama, Mama! Tell Mable she'll ruin her blue dress if she wears it today," Frances needled superiorly.

Mattie removed the dress from Mable's vicelike grip. "Let's go upstairs and pick out one of yer calicos," Mama instructed. "Ya wouldn't want yer new dress t' get dirty or torn. Think of all you'll be doin' at the fair."

"No!" Mable stormed. Her face was becoming the color of her flame-kissed mane. Hot tears bathed her freckles. "My blue dress! My blue dress! I want to be the prettiest girl at the fair."

Mattie was getting nowhere against the fiery iron will of her 5-year-old. She owned no more blue-silk fabric to make a replacement if Mable's Sunday dress was spoiled.

Then she hatched up a plan.

"OK, Mable, ya kin wear yer dress. Let's wrap 'er up in tissue paper and put 'er in a box. We'll put the box under th' seat in th' wagon so it won't git dirty from th' muddy roads on the way. Then, after we git t' the fair, ya kin change into it 'fore ya git out of th' buggy."

Mable seemed content with that proposal, so she donned her calico outfit as Mama instructed. "Just 'till we get there," she sniffled to Mama.

"Just 'till we get thar," Mattie echoed approvingly.

The girls bounced and chattered as the team navigated the

six miles from Brushy Mound into their county-seat town. Bonnie, Frances, and Mable hatched up more ideas about what they could do during the big event. Mattie kept a firm hold on her entry in the relish-making contest. The box containing the blue dress rested against her heels and out of her youngest's line of vision.

Eyes widened with wonder as the Miller family's wagon pulled into the fairgrounds after the one-hour trip into town. A clown with a big red nose stood at the ticket booth and greeted fairgoers. When he spotted the three girls as their Papa hitched the wagon, he began waving. "Welcome, ya pretty young ladies," the grinning clown called out to them.

"Oh, Mama, there's the sign for the food judging," Bonnie noticed. "Let's get your chow-chow over there quick. You might win the blue ribbon." She reached out to take Mama's treasured package while Mama navigated the wagon step.

"I see the cotton-candy booth," Mable shouted exuberantly. "Papa! Give me a nickel. Let's get over there." Her red pigtails bobbed over her green calico as she tugged on Papa's sleeve excitedly.

"I will if ya say the magic word," Papa reminded her.

"Pl-e-e-ease, will you take me to the cotton-candy stand?" Mable replied as she remembered her manners.

Papa led Mable by the hand; the two of them struck off determinedly in the direction Mable indicated. Bonnie and Frances skittered behind them.

Mattie glanced over her shoulder at the long-forgotten bundle that remained untouched under the wagon seat. She smiled knowingly. Mable's green calico would be quite adequate for all the activities of her day. Mattie wisely knew that the blue-silk Sunday dress would never be given another thought.

* * * * * * * *

That the Miller girls would want to be around anything that would even HINT of cotton was amazing, considering all the hours they spent over the cotton rows near their home.

With their picker sacks tossed over their shoulders, the girls would spend hours following their Papa up and down the cotton rows. In those days cotton was the chief source of income for rural families who lived off the black, fertile soil of Northeast Texas. During "pickin' season" even the youngest child was recruited to help "bring home the bacon" for the cotton harvest.

Frances loved to recall how, at day's end among the cotton rows, her picker bag always was the fullest of any gatherer. In her senior years Frances entertained with tales of how she could strip the bolls the cleanest of anyone and earned the title of "cham-peen picker"—at least among her family. "We'd pick until our hands were raw," she often would reminisce to her contemporary audience, who loved her yarns but who could hardly relate to such back-breaking labor.

The Miller girls forgot their blistered fingers when they hauled their bulging sacks to the cotton gin and watched Papa empty the contents into a large tube which suctioned the cotton away for the next stage in the production process. After their work was done, Papa would let the girls stand with their heads near the elevated suction tube. Their hair "went straight up", as Frances laughingly described it decades later.

Three fiery manes that normally cascaded in waves past their shoulders and that now swooshed up to stand highway-stripe straight over their scalps must have been a sight to behold! As Frances would tell it, this bit of entertainment was the sisters' little reward at the end of a long day of toiling alongside the adults in the fields.

* * * * * * * *

A sleepy, copper-topped head nodded against Mama's arm late that afternoon as the team rocked its cargo over the rutted country roads and home from the fair. The Three Red-Haired Miller Girls were bushed after lollygagging all over the fairgrounds.

While Mable snoozed, a subdued Bonnie and Frances took turns fingering ruffles on the fancy ribbon that Mama had garnered for her prize chow-chow.

"Why isn't it blue, Mama?" Bonnie wondered out loud. "I had hoped you would win first prize."

Mama beamed proudly. "Th' white one thar is even better'n a blue," she answered her eldest. "My jar was voted th' best of all the vegetable entries!"

"Why don't we get to bring your chow-chow home if it was best in the contest?" Frances asked.

"Th' judges ate 'er all up," Mama answered her. "That's how they knew it should win the prize for best-of-show. Besides, thar's plenty more chow-chow on th' shelf at home."

A different item wrapped in newspaper and tied with string rested in Mama's lap for the trip back to Brushy Mound. It was Mable's treasure from the fair—a clear-stemmed juice glass that Papa won for her in the coin toss.

Throughout the rest of her childhood—long after she outgrew her blue-silk Sunday dress that she had cried so much to wear—Mable would drink her morning prune juice in her precious fair souvenir.

When Mable had a daughter, that daughter drank her morning prune juice from the same glass as well.

By the time Mable's daughter had a daughter to drink from the juice glass, parents didn't give kids morning prune juice much any more to cleanse their "systems", but the story of how Grandma's daddy won the glass at the fair went equally as well with Katie's favorite breakfast-time drink of SunnyD.*

*SunnyD, or Sunny Delight, is the trademarked name of a popular orange-flavored breakfast beverage.

County Fair Chow-Chow

1 gallon chopped cabbage
1 gallon diced tomatoes
6 large onions, chopped
6 green peppers, chopped
1 or 2 hot peppers, chopped

Put all ingredients into a large kettle; add a handful of salt. Add water just to cover the ingredients. Cover kettle and allow the ingredients to sit overnight while the salt absorbs. Next morning drain off liquid.

To the above mixture stir in:
1 cup sugar
1/2 gallon vinegar
1 tablespoon mustard seed
1 teaspoon celery seed

Tie a little pickling spices into a cheesecloth bag; add to mixture in kettle. Cook all on stove until the mixture is tender. Remove cheesecloth bag. Pour mixture into pint jars that have been sterilized; seal jars. Process in boiling-water bath. Makes about 8 pints.

Chapter 3
Five Women in a House

When, at age 20, I married Louis, I could cook only a scant, few items. As I grew up, if I so much as thrust one big toe into the kitchen to offer to help, my mother shooed me out by shrugging, "Go on. I can do it a lot quicker."

Some assessed that this was a logical byproduct of my rearing as a *spoiled-brat only child.*

Mother and I both knew better. Mable banished me from underfoot because she had spent part of her young adulthood as one of "five women in a house." She was more than happy to have undisputed reign over her present kitchen.

* * * * *

The Three Red-Haired Miller Girls' mama, Mattie, was acclaimed for her outstanding skills as a seamstress—a talent matched only by her amazing cooking. When the Miller Girls were growing up in Brushy Mound, and later, as they moved into town to Cooper, when Mable was in the sixth grade and Bonnie and Frances were in high school, the Miller home was the scene for frequent parties organized on a whim.

The Miller Girls' friends would locate Mark Miller returning home from the field, and later, in town, from his work at the lumber yard.

"Mr. Mark, can we have a party at your house?" they would query, according to Mable, who years later recalled the time.

"Suits me, but y'll hav'ta ask Mattie," he replied.

"We already talked to Miss Mattie, and she said *yes*," was heard the youthful counter.

Young people who surrounded the Miller Girls always knew the answer ultimately would be affirmative and always knew the food would be good, whether it was garden-fresh or some other yield from Mattie's hands.

Friends of Mable, especially, numbered many. Those who autographed her commencement album from the Class of 1930, Cooper High School, testified to her popularity.

"There is not another girl in high school that smiles as much as you do. I can't see how anybody could be blue around you because of your smiles and cheerful ways," wrote one of her fans at graduation time.

Another admirer called her "one of the liveliest girls in school." Another: "I want my little girl to have hair and eyes just like yours." Many who signed her album referenced her red locks. One called her "a little red-headed girl without a temper." A classmate wished her well by writing: " Hoping you get your man."

Beyond her outgoing ways, an even more consistent theme was Mable's intelligence and academic prowess.

From a fellow senior: "I will always remember you as the brightest spot in the class." Class President Willie Smith lauded her "scholarly attitude".

A teacher praised her as "a good, cheerful student".

Her scholarship led her to become the salutatorian of the CHS senior class.

Yet, despite this academic resumé, no mention in her album is made to her pursuing higher education. College in her future gets no reference whatsoever. The presumption was that she would leave high school and immediately begin employment.

One who signed her commencement book wrote:

"Here's to the girl with tresses of red and eyes of a liquid brown.
She's sure to win in the world of work as well as wear beauty's crown."

A teacher penned to Mable: "Soon you will have a lovely position and make good. I know you will."

A *lovely position* in the *world of work* is all that is foreseen for Mable, despite her good grades and industrious pursuit of learning. Most graduating high school in Cooper in those days did not have the economic means to consider college. This was regrettable since East Texas State Normal College (later known as East Texas State University and now a part of the Texas A&M system) was only 15 miles down the road in Commerce.

Truthfully this college might still have been in Cooper, where it was founded in 1889 by William Mayo, had it not been destroyed by fire in 1894. When it was rebuilt, the school was relocated in Commerce, where it remained.

My dad, Doyce Wheeler, whom Mable would marry in 1941, pronounced that the trouble with attending college in Commerce wasn't as much about economics as it was about poor roads. "The roads from Cooper to Commerce were deplorable in those days," he would recall. "To make that daily commute from Cooper over those awful muddy roads was just not possible."

Doyce, like Mable, always considered himself to be college material. In this arena he may have fallen to the misfortune of being second-born. The Wheelers enrolled Doyce's older brother, Buford, at the University of Texas in Austin after Buford's senior year at Cooper High. Buford moved from

Cooper to Austin to pursue college life. But one semester without passing grades and he returned home.

Doyce quoted his mother, Zella, as saying ruefully, "I'll never send another one." Despite his dreams of being college-bound, Doyce (two years Buford's junior) could not persuade his parents otherwise. He thus followed his dad's and brother's line of work in the postal system. To his last years my dad sorrowed that he hadn't been given a chance as a college student.

* * * * * * * *

Mable did locate what in Cooper was considered a *lovely position*—at least a respectable one. She cheerfully hired on as a clerk in Perry Brothers variety and then Perkins dry goods, both on the Cooper Square.

In these jobs she learned to fold clothing items with military precision—a talent that carried into the remainder of her life. My mother bragged on herself that she could pack more items into a suitcase or into the trunk of a car than could any other human being. Our son, Matthew, later joked that he graduated from the "Mable Wheeler School of Packing" because he believed he acquired his grandma's trait.

Getting the most dishes in a dishwasher and thus economizing on fuel and liquid detergent was another of her claims to fame.

When family gathered at Mable's one year, Frances was heard storming from Mable's kitchen in a bit of a huff.

"I *know* no one can pack a dishwasher as tightly as you," Frances blared as she plopped herself down in a chair in the den and fumed there for the duration of the visit.

Other than her giftedness for packing, Mable later remarked that her years of standing on hard floors as she serviced customers netted her nothing but varicose veins. Like my dad, Mother was always a little wistful about being denied any college chances. Of course, like many other members of her generation, Mable was determined to see to it that her own offspring had every opportunity in terms of higher education. *College* was whispered into my ear from my very first conscious moment. My mother would have busted her buttons to have seen her own granddaughter in 2009 receive the highest college degree possible for an individual—the Ph.D., when our Katie became Dr. Katie Welch at the University of Texas at Arlington.

Once asked what course of study she might have pursued as a collegiate, Mable replied, "I always loved history. I probably would have run for political office." None of us doubted that, since she and my dad exhausted themselves in working for Republican political candidates for the remainder of their days.

* * * * * * * *

The most notable takeaway from Mable's employment for the 11 years between high school and her marriage to my dad was support for her widowed mom.

When Mark Miller's sudden passing from a heart condition left Mattie alone in the world at age 50, the Miller Girls knew what was required of them.

"We had our responsibilities," Frances later would say of the era that ultimately saw five women live under the roof of Mattie's Cooper house.

Frances' income was derived as a bank clerk and county extension clerk (described in the next chapter). Bonnie, who by 1940 was living at home with her daughter, Yvonne, after her marriage to Yvonne's dad ended, apprenticed under Mattie as a seamstress. The two women sewed prolifically and gorgeously outfitted many a Cooper lady and man.

Usually the five women (Mattie, her three grown daughters, and Yvonne) lived in a rented dwelling in town. Cooking and cleaning responsibilities were shared. Yvonne was an elementary school child and away from home during the day. She was 11 by the time Mable and Frances each married in 1941.

After she graduated from Cooper High School Class of 1947, Yvonne was the family's first college attendee as she commuted to Commerce for a year. Ultimately, however, she began seeing a dashing suitor—a slightly older Cooper guy and returning military man who had served the 8th Air Force as a flight crew member on B-24 bombers in World War II.

Frances remembered Yvonne's unbridled euphoria as this courtship began. "I *always* wanted to have a date with Joe Choate," Frances (into old age) recalled Yvonne extolling after this love match began to bloom. (And to think that Yvonne won Joe's heart even before he had a chance to sample Yvonne's inimitable Cinnamon Apples, page 91.)

Bonnie's marriage to Bill in 1946 and her joining him at his farm home six miles outside of Cooper took the last two boarders away from Mattie's house in town. Five Women in a House had dwindled to one. For the rest of her days until she moved to a nursing center Mattie lived alone in a quiet that must have roared after the roof once sheltered herself plus the female companionship of Three Red-Haired Miller Girls (and a grandgirl).

One thing never changed: Mattie's good cooking. Though she no longer pursued her own garden, she never lost her touch for preparing those garden-fresh vegetables. Baked Stuffed Onions (on the next page) is but one more example.

Baked Stuffed Onions

6 large onions
1/2 cup grated Cheddar cheese
1 cup Medium White Sauce (see below)
1/2 cup buttered bread crumbs (brown fine, dry crumbs in 2 tablespoons melted butter)
dash paprika

Medium White Sauce:
2 tablespoons butter
2 tablespoons all-purpose flour
1 cup milk

Peel onions whole. Boil in large amount of salt water until tender (10-15 minutes). Drain and rinse in cold water; cut off top of onion and remove center to form a hollow cup. Chop portions removed from centers. For Medium White Sauce: In a separate small pan melt butter; add flour and milk. Cook until thickened. Season to taste. Add cheese. Fill onions with cheese mixture and top with buttered crumbs. Bake at 350 degrees for 25-30 minutes. Remove from oven. Sprinkle with paprika.

Chapter 4

Downtown

When Frances graduated from Cooper High School, she immediately began employment in the county extension office. Her worksite was the massive Delta County Courthouse that dominated the square in downtown Cooper. The county agent visited rural homes in the surrounding area and gave practical, useful tips for farmwives to maximize the yield from their gardens. As a clerk in the extension office Frances typed the recipes for the county agent to take along on visits. (The recipe for Sauteed Okra, Corn, and Tomatoes on page 36 is an example of one Frances might have typed.) As a result Frances had access to many outstanding recipes that went into the file she was building for when she would one day marry and have a home of her own.

Across the square from the bank, on the west corner, was Cooper's First National Bank. One day Mr. Bartley from the bank arrived at the county extension office and asked Frances whether he might speak to her boss. Frances had an outbreak of goosebumps as Mr. Bartley walked into her boss' office and shut the door; had she done something wrong that Mr. Bartley was reporting to the county agent?

However, just the opposite was the case. The bank official told the county agent that he knew Frances was a diligent worker and said he would like to employ Frances to work as a bank teller. Frances was surprised but pleased at this development. Although she loved her current job, in high school she had excelled in her bookkeeping and accounting courses. As a teller she would get to use these skills. Her gregarious personality and her ability to make friends easily would mesh well with the role of meeting and greeting the public as people transacted their bank business. Her boss was sad to lose this valuable employee but gave permission for her to move across the square to the new job.

Once she settled into her banking role, Frances' favorite customer was none other than Grandma Harris. Regally the elderly woman would arrive in the bank lobby wearing her hat, gloves, and a crisply ironed dress. On her lapel she usually wore a brooch featuring a mother-of-pearl base and the name *Frances* decoratively formed on it with woven gold wire. Frances always admired the pin, which had been given Grandma by Grandpa Harris. Later Grandma Harris would bequeath this pin to Frances. Besides Uncle Bert's daughter, Mary Frances, Frances Miller was the only one among all of Grandma Harris' many granddaughters to bear the name of this family matriarch, so naturally she would be the one honored with the keepsake.

Grandma Harris would wait for the line at Frances' teller window to thin out because she trusted only her granddaughter to take care of her money. Grandma made regular visits to deposit Grandpa's military pension from his having served in the Civil War. Most people likely presumed that Joseph Harris had been a Confederate soldier, since Delta County, TX, was decidedly part of the South and his wife, who was born and reared in Mississippi, was a staunch Southern lady through and through.

Truthfully Joe Harris had served as an Army private in the Civil War but represented the Union, not the South. A native of Nashville, IL, he enlisted in the 49th Illinois infantry. After the Civil War he moved to Kaufman County, TX, where Frances' family had moved from Mississippi. The two met there and married. Their different origins may have made for some lively pillow talk for Grandpa and Grandma Harris, but any philosophical differences they might have had were kept between the two of them. None of the Miller girls remembers ever having heard their grandparents discussing the sad and bloody national conflict that so recently had pitted the North against the South.

As in many other county seat towns in those days, the Cooper square was the "happenin' place", especially on Saturday nights. Mable often told about getting off work from her dry-goods store job on Saturday night and spending the rest of the evening simply strolling around the square just to see who else happened to be strolling around that evening.

* * * * * * *

Not far from the square was another "happenin' place" — the train depot. Since cars still were not common in that day and most people did not own their own vehicles, people relied on trains as the major transportation to get from city to city.

Out of that train station, my dad, Doyce Wheeler (known later as J.D.), and his dad, also named J.D., left on one of the most crucial train rides either would ever make — the train that carried the two to Austin for my dad to undergo painful rabies shots after he was bitten by a mad dog. At age 5 Doyce and his brother, Buford, were playing under the porch of their home when a rabid dog hiding there surprised them and took a hunk out of Doyce's abdomen. One look at the dog's glazed eyes and frothing mouth and Doyce's parents knew their son's life was in danger. His dad cut off the dog's head, wrapped it in newspaper, and stuffed it in a pail, which they carried with them on the train to Austin, the only location in the state in which the rabies vaccine was dispensed in that day.

As they embarked on the long and fearful journey, my granddad could not be sure that he would be bringing his younger son back alive. After he received two dozen injections to the stomach and endured much pain that as an elderly man he still could recall in detail, doctors released the boy for his dad to take him back to Cooper. I can only imagine the relief that must have encompassed them on that return trip home—and the raw fear that must have seized my grandmother, Zella, as she waited back in Cooper not knowing the outcome.

The fact that rabid dogs were so common in those days infused everyone with a primal sense of panic about dogs in general. Frances recalls being deathly frightened of any dog she encountered—a fear she carried with her into adulthood. So when her husband, Herbert, brought a tiny spitz named Judy home as a companion for Frances, Frances was ill-at-ease with the puppy and was reluctant to even touch her or be in the same room with her.

Patiently Herbert taught Frances how to relax and enjoy their new pet. Ultimately Frances became so attached to this winsome white furball that Judy became almost like a daughter to this childless couple. Herbert, an inveterate amateur photographer, took photos of Judy in every conceivable pose—propped up by the piano as though she were Liberace, begging for a treat, and even kneeling in a "prayer" posture. In every photo the playful Judy always seemed to be smiling—even laughing. Frances often told about a friend who, in speaking to Judy affectionately, called her, "Judy, you little human dog."

Within two days of her last week of life, Frances was still telling "Judy" stories with amazing clarity. We never related any feat that our bichon, Jack, performed without Frances offering an even more laudatory story about the incomparable, intelligent Judy. Once for Aunt Frances' birthday I framed a grouping of photos of Judy and used a mat that featured numerous photo openings in an oval shape. I hung it directly outside her door at her assisted-living residence. A friend who walked down the hallway and spotted the framed photos queried Frances, "Just how many dogs did you have, anyway?" Frances answered that all the photos were of one dog—beloved Judy, whom she had swathed in love and for whom she mourned disconsolately when Judy ultimately had to be put to sleep.

Eventually Frances and Herbert went on to adopt Mickey, a wirehair terrier who gave birth to Lucky and Lady. Later, as protection for them after an intruder forced his way in on Uncle Herbert in their Lake Highlands home, he and Frances acquired Twiggy, a giant black Doberman with whom no one would ever want to wrangle.

But it was Judy to whom Aunt Frances lost her heart and who would be eulogized full-bore alongside Frances some 70 years later at Frances' funeral service. Surely no more enduring bond between human and beast ever existed on this earth. Those of us who had grown up on "Judy" tales felt sad for the newest generation of littlest family members who would never have the experience of watching Aunt Frances' eyes dance as she described the inimitable dog who was the next step down from being human.

Sauteed Okra, Corn, and Tomatoes

2 pounds fresh okra, with stems and tips removed
3 pounds tomatoes, skinned and seeded
8 ears fresh corn (or 4 cups frozen corn kernels)
2 tablespoons butter
2 tablespoons oil
4 cups onions, coarsely chopped
1 tablespoon salt
freshly ground pepper

Cut okra into 1/4-inch rounds; discard tops. This should make about 6 cups of okra. Put tomatoes in stainless or enameled pan and cook slowly for about half an hour. Do not scorch. Drain any liquid. This should make about 2 cups of tomatoes. Use sharp knife to cut corn from cob, or defrost frozen corn. In a skillet heat butter and oil. Add okra and onions. Cook until onions are wilted and okra has begun to brown at edges, about 10-15 minutes. Turn often; add reduced tomatoes and salt; cook 5 minutes. Add corn and cook 3-4 more minutes. Add salt and pepper; season to taste.

Chapter 5

In the Garden Alone

From pillar to post, pillar to post.
That's how my mother described her first 10 years of marriage to my dad. Their wedded life may have been the rock of stability, but their early living arrangements were like quicksand.

With a sizeable chunk of U.S. males overseas and construction materials all going to the World War II effort, in those days few new homes were being built in the U.S. Couples rented rooms in existing dwellings. Often they had a bedroom of their own but had to share a kitchen, living area, and sometimes even the bathroom with the homeowner and other tenants.

My parents' first love nest was a rented room in the home of Mrs. Texie Tomlinson, a widow who lived on North Eleventh Street near downtown Garland. Mrs. Tomlinson, known as "Aunt Tex", kept a talkative parrot who somewhat disconcertingly squawked out "Hello, Mable" every time my mother walked by.

Mable and J.D.'s march to find permanent quarters took them in a patchwork pattern all over Garland. My mother was quick to bemoan, "I moved three times within nine months." Successive landlords leased to them and then almost instantly sold the houses out from under them as returning G.I.'s needed homes for their families.

When my parents ferried me from the hospital after they

adopted me when I was 3-days old, they lived in a rented room in the Elkins home on Avenue E in Garland. The house wasn't spacious, but my mother recalled obsessing because she lived in fear of the social worker's visit. She was terrified that the social worker for the state would discover dust bunnies multiplying under her bed and therefore blackball her as an unfit mother for her infant. Knowing my mother's penchant for neatness, her horror seems laughable now, but for adoptive couples who almost universally fear they somehow won't measure up, it's never a joking matter.

After the next cottage—on Maple Street—we landed on Resistol Drive. This home featured the screened-in front porch on which I got my head stuck between the seat and the backrest of a wicker rocking chair. My Nanny (Mable's mother, Mattie), who was keeping me that day, frantically yelled for a plumber working next door to free me. As soon as the plumber disappeared and Nanny returned to the kitchen, I repeated the stunt. This was the only time in my life gentle Nanny ever raised her voice at me. By the time my parents arrived home, she was a veritable Vesuvius of frustrations about the event. I'm surprised she didn't string me up by my toenails.

When at last my parents saved up enough for a new home, my mother knew exactly the place she wanted them to buy. It was a lot on 11th Street—just down from their newlywed rented room. My parents wanted to live in a place from which their daughter—then 2 1/2—ultimately could walk to elementary school, junior high, and high school. The 11th-Street property was within a very short distance of all three. Mother called Louise Hunt, who taught at Garland High School while my mother had been secretary there, to see whether Louise's elderly parents would sell the 11th-Street lot which adjoined their home.

Louise's reply wasn't promising.

"Daddy has his fruit orchard and his garden on that lot," Louise advised my mother. "His gardening brings him a great deal of enjoyment."

My parents were sad but looked elsewhere. Although it ran a distant second on their wish list, my parents located another parcel of land—on 5th Street, further away from schools but still near downtown Garland.

On their way to close on this property, their telephone rang.

"Mable, Daddy has decided that he will sell you the lot next door after all," Louise Hunt reported. "He's getting up in years and really doesn't need to be fiddling around with that garden any more."

What music to my parents' ears! Somehow they wriggled out of the other contract and began building a small, gray, frame house on the site that had won their hearts long before.

Most of the garden and orchard that "Brother" Hunt, a retired Baptist minister, had cultivated remained undisturbed by our house's construction. In our front yard was a splendid peach tree that furnished "breakfast" for me anytime I wanted to pick its yield. In our back yard was a little plum tree that had sweet fruit ripe for an afternoon snack in the summer.

Just before we moved in, Brother Hunt had planted onion sets which he left for our family to pick and enjoy. Early every morning before my dad left for work, Daddy would walk his "inherited" garden rows to see how the onions and the garden's other yield were faring.

In church I had just learned the hymn, "I Come to the Garden Alone". As I watched him silently survey the rows in the dewy, early morn, I developed the notion that that hymn was written exclusively for my dad. (Years later we had it sung at his funeral service.) To me this seemed, as the hymnwriter attested, a perfect time to commune with God.

One morning I walked with him. As he passed the onion sets, I bent down to pull a whole onion from the ground and started to stuff it—dirt and all—into my mouth.

"Oh, don't do that!" my dad protested as he grabbed the filthy object from my hand. "You'll be very sorry if you bite into a raw onion."

Naturally, after he'd left for work, I couldn't wait to return to the garden and take that forbidden bite.

Yow! I yelled and then sputtered as the chunk of raw onion caused my mouth to flame. Daddy had been right, of course. I never again repeated that little rebellious act that for hours later left my mouth a lit torch.

* * * * * * * *

The proximity to our new neighbors, the Hunts, fostered an instant friendship between me and the venerable Brother Hunt, who was in his 80s and enjoyed having a small, inquisitive visitor around.

Often my mother would send me through the opening in the garden hedge dividing the two properties and onto the Hunts' back porch, where I would borrow a cup of sugar, a cup of flour, or an egg for my mother's baking.

Those visits found me lingering at the Hunts', where Brother Hunt—by then a semi-invalid—persuaded me to sing a song or listen to his jokes.

The Hunts were generous almost to a fault. I learned very quickly that if I merely complimented something in the Hunt residence—be that a bow on a potted plant from the florist or a knickknack within my line of vision—I almost always was sent home with it. I'm sure my mother feared I was a klepto in the making; the Hunts were often phoned to reassure her that they eagerly had loaded me up with the gift.

Daughter Louise, a single woman who lived with her parents and cared for them, enjoyed showing me a photograph of her father as a young man. The photo hung in the back porch room of my frequent visits. It pictured her dad as a seminary student while he trained for the ministry. I was fascinated to see old Brother Hunt, now with white hair and stooped carriage, as a mustachioed young man in his prime. I stared at this photo for hours as I stood in this back-porch hallway. If I had ever indicated the slightest interest, I'm sure the Hunts would have immediately ripped it off the wall and bequeathed it to me right then as well. (Later on, one Hunt grandson did just that. That photo of the 1900 graduating class of the Southern Baptist Theological Seminary now hangs in my home.)

With their own grandchildren older and living out of town, I became this elderly couple's entertainment. One Halloween when Brother Hunt was recovering from a mean case of the shingles, my mother insisted that I bypass the Hunt house on my rounds of trick-or-treating.

I was back home and already out of my Halloween regalia when the phone rang.

"Isn't Kay stopping by?" Louise Hunt inquired on the other end. "Daddy was waiting up for her. He didn't want to go to bed until he saw her in her Halloween outfit."

Quickly I was re-attired and hustled off to ring the Hunts' front doorbell. Brother Hunt was in ecstasy as he plunked some candy into the bag of a wee, costumed skeleton.

Ultimately death crept up on old Brother Hunt's body. I made my last trip through the garden-hedge opening and said goodbye to my octogenarian friend.

"Brother Hunt will be going to heaven soon," his daughter told me as I stepped onto the familiar back porch.

The idea of Brother Hunt walking the Streets of Gold intrigued me. I could envision him strolling heaven's Hall of Fame. Because he had been a preacher, I was sure he'd have conversations with Bible characters. He might even practice his jokes on them.

Then it dawned: he'd be seeing Teddy Roosevelt! Wow!

T.R. was my major childhood heroes. I read his biographies and even corresponded with one of his living children. What an opportunity for Brother Hunt! He'd be in the company of this legendary former President as well.

"Will you do me a favor?" I piped as I stood by the bedside of this failing, lovable neighbor.

"Of course," he whispered.

"When you get to heaven, will you tell Teddy Roosevelt hello for me?"

At that brazen utterance, my mother clapped her hand over my mouth. Who says such things to a dying man?

Brother Hunt didn't act as though my request was untoward at all.

"Why, of course I will," he replied feebly but managing a slight smile.

I was certain Brother Hunt would carry out my wishes. After all, at the Hunt house I always got exactly what I asked for.

* * * * * * * *

My parents' little gray frame home—with the peach tree in the front and the plum tree in the back—ultimately gave way to a three-bedroom, two-bath, two-car-garage, brick home typical of the 1960s on the front of their 11th-Street lot. The gray house out back remained as the office for my mother's typing and mailing service, while the modern, salmon-colored brick one became our residence. My mother often commented that 11th Street had been "magic" for her and my dad. On this street they began their marriage in one rented room. In their spacious, brick, dream home on 11th Street they went on to celebrate 52 years of wedded life.

The garden in which my daddy walked alone while the dew was still on the roses ultimately was plowed under so a gorgeous carpet of St. Augustine could grow.

Years later I discovered a recipe for Plum-Peach Crumble. Smiling as I recalled those two trees that once flanked my early childhood dwelling, I baked that dessert with the sweetest of memories.

Plum-Peach Crumble

1/4 cup brown sugar
1/2 cup granulated sugar
1/2 teaspoon salt
1/2 stick butter
1/2 cup all-purpose flour
1/2 teaspoon cinnamon
1/4 teaspoon baking powder
1 egg
1/4 cup granulated sugar
1 egg
1/2 cup heavy cream (can substitute skim milk or
   2-percent milk)
1 teaspoon almond extract
3/4 pound plums, peeled and chopped
3/4 pound peaches, peeled and chopped
whipped topping and slivered almonds

Mix together brown sugar, 1/2 cup granulated sugar, and salt. Cut in butter until mixture resembles coarse meal. Stir in flour. Divide mixture in half. Set one-half aside. To other half add cinnamon, baking powder, and 1 egg. Blend well. Press into bottom of 9-inch square pan. Bake at 350 degrees for 5 minutes. While crust bakes, whisk together remaining 1/4 cup sugar, 1 egg, cream (or milk), and almond extract. Remove crust from oven and spread chopped plums and peaches on top. Pour cream mixture over fruit. Sprinkle with reserved half of butter-flour mixture. Sprinkle with additional brown sugar if desired. Bake until crumb topping is browned, at 350 degrees for about 15 minutes. Serve warm with whipped topping and almonds.

Chapter 6
A Cake Never Baked

For a child growing up in the 1950s, traveling across Dallas from my Garland home to Aunt Frances' house in Oak Cliff seemed somewhat akin to trekking to the moon.

In the days before Interstate 30 zipped through Dallas, our complicated route took us snaking by Garland's "Miracle Mile" of auto dealerships, meandering past White Rock Lake, weaving around through the overpowering downtown skyscrapers, and inching over the Trinity River viaduct with its arches and quaint lampposts.

Once we crawled into Oak Cliff, a Dallas suburb which contained the only actual "cliff", or hill, that I ever experienced in my city on the plains, we at last found Aunt Frances' modified Craftsman-style bungalow in a quiet neighborhood on Montreal Street.

The 90-minute trip, which today could be knocked out in a half-hour flat via speedy I-30, seemed endless to a school-aged child. But I knew of few other places on earth I'd rather be than in the home of this childless, doting aunt.

I loved every part of Aunt Frances' house, starting with her coffee table that contained the most captivating candy dish I'd ever seen. Its milky white lid was inset with slices of crystal blue glass and had hand-painted gold flowers adorning it. Although I was born with an insatiable sweet tooth, I was far more caught up in examining the glory of Aunt Frances' candy jar than I was in checking out its sugary contents.

I also adored standing in her kitchen with its knotty pine paneling. It effused warmth and coziness and seemed a place highly conducive to good things simmering on the stove. In that kitchen on one particular visit, Aunt Frances and I assembled ingredients to bake her a cake for her 52nd birthday celebration the next day on April 12. Because the strawberry patch in her backyard garden always yielded a profundity of sweet berries, Aunt Frances liked a particular strawberry cake recipe. We had just returned from grocery shopping and were setting her mixing bowls, spoons, and measuring cups out onto the counter so we could begin work on that project.

But cake preparation was stopped cold that afternoon by an unexpected phone call. As Aunt Frances spoke to the caller—a friend of my mother's—her voice suddenly dropped to hushed level.

"Oh, you don't say," I heard her intone quietly. "It just happened? Oh, I'm so sorry. Well, thank you for letting me know. I'll phone Mable right now."

My eyes must have held a million question marks, but Aunt Frances turned and reported news to me that my 10-year-old gut had already sensed—my Mammaw had died just minutes before. Only yesterday my mother had telephoned us that my dad's mom seemed to be rallying from the heart attack she had sustained earlier that week. Mother and Daddy had brought me over to stay with Aunt Frances and Uncle Herbert for the weekend so my parents could give their full attention to Mammaw in the hospital.

But my grandmother's delicate little body was too weak to make much progress against the crippling blow to her cardiovascular system. Several nights beforehand my parents had taken me to the hospital to see Mammaw. She had worn an oxygen mask—not the nose canula and tubing like people on oxygen use today but a sinister, gray, hissing device that covered most of her face and made her look alien. As I haltingly approached her bedside, Mammaw attempted to set me at ease.

"What do you think of my Halloween mask, sweetheart?" she managed in a weak, raspy voice.

I'm not sure what, if anything, I said back. Just before I had entered Mammaw's room, my mother had sternly instructed, "Now don't you start weeping when you go in there." After a few seconds of my gawking at Mammaw in her perplexing mask (and not weeping!), my parents ushered me out. What my parents seemed to fear, I still can't fathom. Wouldn't tears, after all, have been an absolutely appropriate reaction for a little 10-year-old girl in the presence of a beloved grandmother whom she might not see again on this earth?

As things turned out, I indeed *had* laid eyes on Mammaw for the last time. After her Saturday passing, Mammaw's body was returned to her hometown of Cooper, where her funeral service was held the following day. Aunt Frances' 52nd birthday, for which we were to make the Strawberry Layer Cake, was spent with all of us attending the funeral for my grandmother, Zella Wright Wheeler. The next day's scheduled celebration for Aunt Frances quickly was replaced by a time of mourning. We focused on comforting my grieving Banddad as he buried his sweetheart of 55 years.

The following morning, a schoolday for me, I dashed into the kitchen of our home and searched the counter for my familiar breakfast of steaming oatmeal, which my mother always set out for me to find.

But neither my mother nor the oatmeal was present in the kitchen. Instead my mother sat on my grandfather's bedside on the pull-out sofa in our living room, where he had slept for the night instead of returning to his empty home. Her arm was draped around the shoulder of Banddad, who had greeted the morning with sobs as the utter aloneness of his life situation broke over him. I was glad Mother's aversion to tears didn't extend to my bereft granddad. The touching scene made a lifelong impression on me because of the tenderness with which my mother comforted her disconsolate, weeping father-in-law. Because of this modeling, derisive "in-law" jokes never made much sense to me as I grew older and began to hear them.

Another aspect of the experience also marked me indelibly. Even today I am unable to catch the scent of carnations without remembering those that blanketed Mammaw's casket in this, my earliest experience with a family funeral. I can hardly inhale them today without recalling my own desperate, 10-year-old mix of grief and confusion that permeated that time.

Though utterly lost in his sudden widowhood, despondency did not reign forever for Banddad. Three years later he eloped with a snowy-haired, never-wed nurse whom he met while visiting church friends. His second wife, Ruth, provided him almost 20 years of companionship (and built-in nursing care, since she took his blood pressure every day).

When Banddad finally passed away just six months shy of his 100th birthday, he had enjoyed many satisfying years beyond that raw morning when he wept forlornly at his bedside and believed his life was over for sure.

* * * * * * * *

Aunt Frances may have traded a strawberry cake for funeral gloom on her 52nd birthday, but she would go on to be served another 50 years of birthday cakes to make up for it.

Many visitors to her retirement home described the white sheet cake with the fluffy white frosting and pink lettering that spelled out, "Happy 102nd Birthday, Aunt Frances," as one of the best they had ever tasted.

Strawberry Layer Cake

1 (18 1/2-ounce) package white cake mix
1 (3-ounce) package strawberry-flavored gelatin
1/2 cup oil
1/2 cup water
3 eggs
10 ounces fresh strawberries, sliced, mashed, and
 drained, reserving juice (can also use 1
 10-ounce package frozen strawberries, thawed)
frosting

Combine cake mix and gelatin. Add oil and water; beat 2 minutes. Add eggs and beat 4 to 5 minutes. Drain strawberries, reserving juice; fold berries into batter. Pour into two greased and floured 9-inch cake pans. Bake at 350 degrees for 40 minutes. Cool in pans 10 minutes. Remove from pans and cool completely. Fill and frost with Frosting (recipe below). Makes one 2-layer cake.

Frosting:
1/2 cup butter, melted
1 (16-ounce) box powdered sugar, sifted
About 1/4 cup reserved strawberry juice

Combine melted butter and powdered sugar. Add enough juice to make a spreading consistency. Beat until fluffy.

Chapter 7

One Smart Indian

In two different parts of the country, long before we ever were to meet, my future husband and I each were experiencing the Quintessential Summer Memory.

After Louis and I began courting and recounted the red-letter events of each of our childhoods, no experience stood out quite like our respective growing-up, summer visits "down on the farm."

For me, of course, that occurred in the Delta County farmhouse of my Aunt Bonnie and Uncle Bill, not far from the Brushy Mound community in which the Three Red-Haired Miller Girls had been young sprouts. In my earlier cookbook, *Way Back in the Country,* I described the sun-dappled mornings of waking up to the reassuring gravel crunch of the milk truck retrieving yesterday's proceeds from Uncle Bill's substantial dairy.

The grade-school bell's final dismissal ring each May brought the glad realization that my annual stay at the farm was just days away. It was the singular event toward which the entire year always marched.

My cousins, Mark and Bill, who were my childhood playmates, joined me each summer as we passed flawless, lazy days making mud pies and using the tailgate of Uncle Bill's green truck as our "pie shop" to pretend to sell our wares.

Secretly I always hoped that my stay included at least one storm, since traipsing down the steps into Aunt Bonnie's storm shelter—its walls lined with her canning jars—was a decided adventure. Aunt Bonnie and her sisters had grown up with Mama's watchful eye on the sky to see if any clouds looked ominous. Bonnie followed suit with her precautions, so the faintest gray cloud sent us scuttling underground. Of course on sunny days my cousins and I found the cellar's above-ground mound to be a lovely ramp for our footraces.

Canning season usually overlapped with my week-long visit, so Aunt Bonnie recruited me as an eager partner to shell and peel and chop. On her back porch with newspapers spread under white wooden, straight-back chairs we sat with pans in our laps and vast sacks of garden yield stuffed between us. The stains on my fingertips from peeling peaches would take the rest of the summer to wear off.

On these glory days, wearing one of my aunt's kitchen aprons, I felt quite adultlike when Aunt Bonnie asked me to join her in this enterprise. A few months later, at Christmas, when Aunt Bonnie's table for our family meal overflowed with some of her garden fare, I drew great delight from bragging to other family members, "I helped!"

Milking time was an experience this city-bred girl certainly didn't have every day. I loved to watch Uncle Bill systematically guide each milk cow into her stall as he lined them up for their nightly duty in his pin-neat dairy barn. Although his herd all looked alike to me, Uncle Bill had a name for each; "Bessie" and "Flossie" and "Della" and the others obediently responded to his gentle call. The *swish-swish* of the milking machines had a comforting rhythm that communicated well-being. Aunt Bonnie and Uncle Bill's world possessed a rich, easy quietude that made all cares seem light-years away.

At night my aunt and uncle generously relinquished their double bed in the front bedroom so I could have the best accommodation in the house. I fell asleep counting the cars' mesmerizing *whir-r-r-r*'s as they breezed by on the state highway outside my window.

* * * * * * * *

Across the Red River in the neighboring state of Oklahoma, my husband-to-be was developing a similar passion for all things country.

Louis recalls his mother's tales of growing up in a family of 11 on the farm outside Norman. As with Aunt Frances' self-description of being "poor but didn't know it", the Mauldin family worked together to be sure plenty of food was put by, with a cellar full of canned goods.

"They had a potato cellar that was separate from the one with canned goods," Louis narrated. In cold weather "the boys"—his mother's brothers—took turns keeping a fire going near the dugout-like cellar so the potatoes wouldn't freeze.

Later, when his mother, Grace, was a young teen, the family moved into Oklahoma City proper, but two-thirds of the Mauldin family yard in town was set aside for a garden and chicken house. After the Mauldin parents passed away and son Bill inherited the home, he turned the plot into a rose garden so the family would have plenty of cut flowers with which to decorate graves on Memorial Day, a mind-boggling tradition unique among Oklahomans.

With this history, the summer ritual of Louis, his brother Robert and sister Mary spending a week at their Aunt Tennie and Uncle W.C.'s acreage in far southwest Oklahoma City was something the Moore children breathlessly awaited as I had my annual Delta County trip.

Besides providing a rural experience, the annual invitation was Tennie's way of helping her sister, Grace, who reared her three children alone as an employed mom, and giving her some free time in the summer without kids always underfoot.

When the Moore niece and nephews arrived, "the first thing we wanted to do was to check out the chicken house and collect eggs," Louis remarks. His Uncle W.C. kept at least a dozen varieties of fowl—including banties, quail, guinea, and chuckers. "We always found eggs, no matter when we arrived." W.C. died in his 50s with the blockage in his carotid artery as thick as library paste; my husband always wondered whether his uncle maxed out on too much cholesterol because of the nearby henhouse.

W.C., an engineer for the F.A.A. at Will Rogers Airport, had laid out his vegetable gardens and fruit-tree orchard methodically, with precision rows of carrots, cabbage, green beans, onions, and tomatoes. "We would go out and collect whatever Aunt Tennie wanted to fix for dinner," my husband related. "Tennie taught school during the year, so gardening and putting up food was her relaxation during the summertime."

Nothing beat preparing fresh fried chicken for dinner, especially when "dinner" had been alive and clucking just one hour earlier, recalled my husband. "W.C. and I would go to the chicken house while he decided which chicken would be the victim," he told. "He would put on gloves, grab a knife, and quickly cut off the head over a chopping block."

The chicken, minus its head, might run around for a few minutes before it gave up the ghost. Nobody thought this chicken-slaughtering drill to be barbaric or "gross". "You just grew up with it," Louis assessed.

W.C., who once helped build the Panama Canal, then would pick up the decapitated chicken by its feet and with it dripping blood all the way would whisk it to the house. Tennie had a pot of water at full boil and newspapers fanned out on the table. She would dip the chicken—feathers and all—into the boiling water.

"Hot water released the feathers," my husband described. "Mary, Robert, and I would pull out the big feathers and the down. Tennie would save the smaller feathers to make pillows."

With a fresh stratum of newspapers now protecting the table, Tennie took her butcher knife, zapped off the feet, and sliced open the belly for the next-most exciting part—removing the "intricals", as she called the *entrails*, to separate out the heart, gizzard, liver, and neck.

"Sometimes we would find a full-fledged egg or an egg without its shell where a shell hadn't formed," Louis described. "We would get to keep the egg."

The Moore kids would help Tennie flour, salt, and pepper the chicken pieces for her to then fry in hot grease on the stove. "It was the freshest chicken you could ever imagine. It was all part of the gardening experience."

* * * * * * * *

But the ties to the American soil that belong to Louis' father's kin go beyond any that I've reported so far in either of our families. They are the most profound of all and trace back to an era before any Anglo set foot on Delta County or Oklahoma or any other U.S. terrain, for that matter.

From Louis' earliest memory his dad talked about his Indian (Native American) heritage but did not tie it to a specific tribe. "He would say that Grandpa Moore (Louis' grandfather, Thomas Nowell Moore, whom Louis never knew) was part Indian, but he didn't seem to discuss many details."

Louis' dad, Louis A. Moore Sr., died when my husband was 16, so by the time the son's curiosity intensified, his dad was not around to interview. After their dad passed away, the children's contact lessened with the Moore extended family for a time.

Louis' mom reflected an attitude that often prevailed among non-Indian residents in the state. "She would razz me that I was so little Indian that I could cut my little finger and all my Indian blood would drain out," he said. His mom—not unlike many other white Anglo-Saxon Protestants—sometimes would use the term "pack of Indians" to refer to some Oklahomans with known Indian blood. She might even throw in the term "dumb Indian" to suggest that someone of that ethnicity wasn't very smart.

Still, Louis realized that on the infrequent occasions when he was around his Moore family relatives, they seemed to speak with gargantuan pride about their Native American roots.

"I presumed they were Cherokee," he said, "Everyone wanted to be Cherokee; they were the tribe that was the best thought-of at that time."

One year at Christmas, after he was an adult, he sent his Aunt Lydia, his father's older sister, a simple, courteous Christmas card. To Louis' amazement his aunt responded with an avalanche of fresh information—furnishing his family's number on the Dawes rolls, the list drawn up between 1898-1907 to determine who was and who wasn't a true member of one of the so-called Five Civilized Tribes. His grandfather, Thomas Nowell Moore, had been an original Dawes enrollee as a Chickasaw. Little did Louis realize how important that one micro-shred of information would be for him and his progeny.

Louis visited the local genealogical library and was able to find and copy his grandfather's original enrollee card. This whetted his yen for greater research. His first effort at sleuthing in the noted Mormon genealogy library in 1986 produced nothing. Then, in 1989, when he visited Salt Lake City again on business, he stopped by the Mormon library to take one more stab. To his astonishment he typed in the name

Thomas Nowell Moore and out poured his entire Indian heritage back to the first Chickasaw squaw who married an English frontiersman.

Three generations down from that squaw, the first Chickasaw to marry a Moore was Catharine Mitchell, the wife of Christopher Moore, another English frontiersman. This husband and wife were the grandparents of Thomas Nowell Moore. According to Mormon records they lived on a 1,000-acre plantation in Northern Mississippi and owned at least three slaves. However, even though she was married to a white man and the duo clearly were people of means, in the late 1830s Catharine and Christopher were forced to move away from Chickasaw ancestral lands in Mississippi in the Removal (also known by the other Civilized Tribes as the "Trail of Tears"). This was the government's effort to take Indian lands in the Southeast United States and exchange them for lesser quality lands in what is now Southern and Eastern Oklahoma.

With all these facts in front of him Louis could see that his mother was correct in a sense; his degree of Indian blood was, some might say, miniscule.

However, his mother thoroughly missed the mark on the "dumb Indian" part. His paternal grandfather, Thomas Nowell Moore, might have just been one of the smartest Indians around.

Some of Tom's contemporaries no doubt were frightened to sign the Dawes Rolls (think Hitler marking the Jews in WW II) or, to say the least, were ashamed to list themselves. They would have died before they would have had their names on any roster that identified the whole kaboodle as Native Americans.

But Thomas Nowell Moore, for whatever reason, signed proudly. Because of this Louis and his siblings ultimately were able to obtain their CDIB (Certificate of Degree of Indian

Blood) and their Chickasaw citizenship cards—all because they can trace themselves to an original Dawes enrollee. Many people may know full well that they have a much higher degree of Indian blood than the Moore siblings do, but if they cannot specifically link with birth and death certificates to an ancestor on the Dawes Rolls, they cannot be legitimized as citizens. (The Chickasaw Nation in recent years eliminated all blood quantums, so a person—no matter how much or how little his degree of blood kin—now is considered just as much Chickasaw as is a full-blood.)

What has this act by one smart Indian meant to Louis, his siblings, and their descendants who know Thomas Nowell Moore only by a signature on a vitally important document?

Only college scholarships, books, computers, and educational incentives for Katie. Only school clothing each semester for my grandchildren. Only free medical care at Chickasaw facilities including the new state-of-the-art medical center in Ada. Only free underground storm shelters and home-improvement stipends. Only trailer-loads of free produce each summer. And those benefits are for Chickasaws who live <u>outside</u> the nation's boundaries in Southern Oklahoma <u>as well as</u> those within the confines of the former reservation.

By the time our daughter, Katie, who is way down the totem pole in terms of blood quantum, graduated in August 2009 with her Ph.D., the Chickasaw Nation had funded at least half of her four-year graduate program and presented her with a gorgeous academic stole noting her heritage.

All this reflects newfound, fortuitous business acumen on the part of the once-beaten-down Chickasaws. Maximizing their resources, the Chickasaws have pulled themselves up by their moccasin laces and now are among America's smaller but more prosperous tribes. As the Chickasaw Nation is investing in its people, who now live all over the world, it is winning undying loyalty from generations yet unborn.

Like Aunt Frances' pronouncement about her farm-nourished family, Louis and his kin "were rich"—rich with a proud Native American heritage that has translated into a vastly more enhanced life than their precursors ever would have dreamed.

Ripped from their comfortable homes by a tragic removal in the mid-19th century, these early Americans—with forebears here long before the white man—experienced hardship and heartache that seem unthinkable today.

But descendants of those persecuted ones now bask in the sunshine of a new day for Native Americans. I am proud to be related to some noble Chickasaws—my husband, son, daughter, and grandchildren—through whose veins course the blood of true American royalty.

The Moores' progenitors were among the bluebloods to whom our country originally belonged.

A great debt to them is in the process of being repaid.

In honor of the Chickasaw Nation I include a recipe for *Three Sisters Stew*, a recipe furnished by the Chickasaw Nation Nutrition Services. In truth, the recipe is named "Three Sisters" because three of its ingredients—corn, yellow squash, and zucchini—typically are all grown near each other in garden rows. However, since this book centers around the lives of the three sisters—the Three Red-Haired Miller Girls—this recipe seemed especially appropriate.

Three Sisters Stew

1 pound ground beef (or ground turkey)
2 cups onions, diced
6 cups water
2 (14 1/2-ounce) cans diced tomatoes
6 cups red-skinned potatoes, cubed
1 (15-ounce) can tomato sauce
1 cup fresh corn kernels, cut from the cob
1 cup yellow squash, diced
1 cup zucchini, diced
1 (15 1/2-ounce) can light red kidney beans, drained and rinsed
1 (15 1/2-ounce) can black-eyed peas, drained and rinsed
1/2 cup quick-cooking barley
4 garlic cloves, minced
1 1/2 teaspoons black pepper

In a skillet on medium-high heat, brown ground beef (or turkey) and onions. Drain meat. In a large kettle add all ingredients. Bring to a boil, then lower heat and simmer for 30-45 minutes until the potatoes are soft. Serve immediately. Makes 12 (1 1/2-cup) servings.

Chapter 8
A Sweet Taste of Victory

Although Aunt Frances' house was clear across Dallas from our little gray frame home in Garland, no one will ever convince me that I had not seen from my own back porch the exact monster funnel cloud that once tore up her Oak Cliff neighborhood.

It wasn't the most powerful nor the deadliest tornado ever, but in the decades since, this legendary 1957 Dallas storm has been labeled one of the most-studied and best-documented tornadoes on record.

Just two blocks away from Aunt Frances' little bungalow on South Montreal, a man was killed as the late-afternoon, F4 twister rumbled up his street and blew his house to bits.

Before the storm's fury fizzled and the cyclone disappeared over Bachman Lake, 10 people in her part of Dallas were dead and more than 200 injured. Damage was set at $4 million.

* * * * * * *

On that afternoon just before the tornado began making its tragic journey through her area, Aunt Frances was entertaining company. Her mother, Mattie, had traveled from Cooper to Dallas for a week-long visit at Frances and Herbert's house. They were about to head out in the car to go shopping. Frances wanted to take Mama to look at some house slippers at the nearby Wynnewood Mall.

Frances and Mattie still would head out in the car, but the leisurely shopping trip would be quickly forgotten. Instead they found themselves making a panicked dash to get out of the way of the killer storm that lurked frighteningly near Frances' own back yard.

* * * * * * * *

On fair-weather days Frances' back yard long had been the scene of some devoted gardening. During World War II Uncle Herbert, like about 20 million other Americans, planted his Victory Garden there. His most memorable yield, according to Frances, consisted of tomatoes the size of grapefruits and large expanses of speckled butterbeans that scaled their cedar fence.

More than six decades later, any mention to Aunt Frances that we were putting up tomatoes from our own backyard garden produced the same automatic comment each time: "Oh, you know, Herbert grew gigantic tomatoes in his Victory Garden during the war."

As war raged overseas, Victory Gardens became a major part of daily life on the home front, as the government called on citizens to reduce the pressure on the public food supply brought on by the war effort. Victory Gardens often were considered civil "morale" boosters, as gardeners could feel empowered by their contribution of labor and rewarded by the produce grown.

For generations farm families had been planting gardens and preserving produce, but this patriotic act saw city-dwellers such as Aunt Frances and Uncle Herbert set aside significant plots in their yards to heed the call to grow their own fruit and vegetables.

A leviathan canning endeavor in Frances' kitchen followed the harvest. Aunt Frances and Olive Rhodes, her lifelong friend and the wife of Herbert's cousin, Baxter, for days on end would labor over batches of stewed tomatoes, butterbeans, and other items. Companionship and girltalk intermingled with the steam of boiling-water baths and the hiss of pressure-cookers as the two women put food by and shared the proceeds. Popular women's magazines of that era gave instructions on how to grow and preserve garden produce. Frances, however, needed no tutoring. She had grown up helping Mama and watching Grandma Harris make gardening and canning a family effort. (A recipe for Butterbeans with Ham follows on page 68. Although different from Frances' canned butterbeans, this is an "old-timey" recipe that definitely uses butterbeans from the garden.)

* * * * * *

While storm clouds amassed over his South Dallas neighborhood on this momentous afternoon of April 2, 1957, Herbert was happily unaware of the massive news story that was unfurling in his own community.

On his day off from work as the operator of the Davis Street Drive-In in Oak Cliff, Herbert headed out with his fishing pole. As on many other days, he found the fish biting in Lake Tawakoni (on whose shores Louis and I later would add a vacation home) 65 miles east of Dallas. Had Frances not been hosting Mama on this April day, she likely would have joined him. A domesticated homebody, Frances never had previously cottoned to fishing, but because it was so much a part of her sweetheart's life, she learned to be a willing partner with rod and reel.

As much as reeling in the fish, Herbert enjoyed exploring the water's edge for specimens of natural driftwood that had washed onto shore. His inventor's eye beheld possibilities most other people missed; thus he envisaged driftwood as an art form. One year he entered in the Texas state fair his collection of mounted driftwood "sculptures" of varying sizes and shapes. Decades later, homes and gardens of his family members proudly exhibit Uncle Herbert's unusual driftwood finds. Craggy, rough-hewn, yet with a unique stripe of appeal, they seem to embody this gravely-throated uncle with the Texas-sized heart.

As he tossed his fishing equipment into his pickup and meandered back toward Dallas on that April afternoon, he noticed the boiling clouds in the distance. Stopping in a roadside diner for some coffee Herbert caught snatches of conversation—truckers discussing a catastrophic tornado that had just plowed through Big D's south side—HIS part of town, where his home and business were.

"He high-tailed it out of there in a flash," 102-year-old Frances recalled on one of our evening visits when we mentioned that Dallas happened to be under a tornado alert that particular day. In seconds she once again spieled off her 54-year-old personal storm story as though it happened yesterday.

Sirens, flashing lights from police cruisers, and blocked-off streets greeted Herbert as he dashed over the Trinity River viaduct into Oak Cliff. Downed trees and masses of debris caused his heart to knock in this dismal hour of lead. What other terrifying sites would he find when he pressed on into the heart of Oak Cliff?

Heading first to the vicinity of his home, he found barricades closing off his residential neighborhood several blocks before he could reach Montreal. At that point he diverted to his workplace, the Davis Street Drive-In, which had just reopened for business after everyone inside had taken cover during the storm. Co-workers told him all they knew, which was little. The city was just beginning to comprehend the magnitude of the event; the men gathered at the drive-in had no way of knowing that the injured were flooding into area hospitals. No one had seen or heard from Herbert's wife nor from any of their spouses either, for that matter. Herbert grabbed the drive-in phone to call Frances, but phone lines were down everywhere.

* * * * * * * *

On that fateful day Oak Cliff's Davis Street was in the center of history because of the tornado that touched down nearby, but Davis Street actually had been a thoroughfare of historic significance many years earlier.

Davis Street originally was part of the Bankhead Highway, the nation's first paved road between Washington, D.C., and San Diego. Commissioned in 1916 it was only the nation's second transcontinental highway.

Interestingly, that section of the old Bankhead in Oak Cliff ultimately linked with the Garland section of the Bankhead, which ran in front of my friend Nan's house. Because of her location on this key artery (now known as Main Street) through downtown Garland, she and I always had a ringside seat on her curb to watch Garland's annual Labor Day Parade, which wound down Bankhead as it headed toward the town square.

Little did I realize that far on the other side of Dallas, Oak Cliff's version of Bankhead was a street that would play a major role in my family's history.

In the Davis Street Drive-In Uncle Herbert installed the

prototype of his new invention, the electric, wood-burning barbecue pit, a cooker that would turn this garden-variety drive-in grocery into the source for world-class barbecue beef. People from all over Dallas and elsewhere soon would be flocking to Davis Street to sample the drive-in's new fare.

By 1959, two years later, Uncle Herbert's barbecue enterprise far outgrew its corner of the Oak Cliff drive-in grocery store. He built a free-standing eatery in the corner of Minyard's supermarket in Mesquite and installed his pit, which would go on to be world-renowned. Ultimately relocated just down the road from its first location, Mesquite BBQ just celebrated 50 years in the business. Uncle Herbert's wooden restaurant chairs with their orange formica dining tops still sit out front to accommodate diners today.

* * * * * * *

But on April 2, 1957, as he grappled to learn about his wife's well-being, his pit that would soon make him a legend in the barbecue business was the last thing on Herbert's mind. At about 8 o'clock that night my uncle finally was able to inch his pickup through the barricades and gain access to his home street of Montreal. Just after letting himself in and finding no apparent damage to his dwelling, he saw the car bearing Frances and Mattie pull into the driveway. Barricades likewise had kept them from returning home for several hours, so they had done as many other Oak Cliff-dwellers did in those frightening minutes after the storm—driven the perimeters of their neighborhoods to try to spot any destruction that might impact them.

A relieved Herbert greeted his spouse and mother-in-law, who recounted the events of their scary afternoon. At about

4:30, when they had looked out the picture window in the living room and seen whirling dirt and debris at ground level at the far end of their street, Frances and Mattie believed they had no choice except to try to flee by car. At this time no neighborhood-level emergency warning system existed, but Mattie had spent their growing-up years tugging her girls into the family's storm shelter with her, so she knew by experience that what she and Frances spotted in the vicinity meant trouble.

Pulling their green-and-cream Chevrolet coupe out of the driveway, Frances could see the funnel cloud more easily. This apparently was the formation that at that time was making its way down nearby Polk Street in a six- or seven-mile northward path. At first the funnel did not reach all the way to the ground, but Frances was able to observe debris periodically spraying up into the air. Before many minutes the tornado would turn deadly. Frances drove frantically in a direction opposite of where she saw the swirling.

Within about 32 minutes, the great Dallas tornado of 1957 finally died. Some estimates say it weenied out for good somewhere near the city limits of Farmers Branch.

* * * * * * * *

Out in Garland reports of what transpired in Oak Cliff was chilling. The 6 p.m. evening news was dominated with on-the-scene reports and footage. Although no reports specifically naming Montreal street were aired, my mother could tell how perilously close targeted spots of damage were to Fran-ces' bungalow and Herbert's business. Anxious evening hours ensued as my mother continued to dial Frances feverishly but reached only a dead phone line. Just down the street from my parents' house was the City of Garland emergency communications center. My mother contacted people there to see if they could locate anyone involved in Oak Cliff disaster response. The communications folks took down her information about Aunt Frances.

Just before my mother tucked me in, a ham-radio operator phoned her. He had managed to get through; Aunt Frances and Nanny were safe at home with Uncle Herbert. Their house was unharmed by the storm.

* * * * * * * *

More than a decade had lapsed since World War II spawned Uncle Herbert's Victory Garden in their back yard, but at Aunt Frances' dwelling where those grapefruit-sized tomatoes once grew was the sweet taste of victory on the evening of April 2, 1957.

Although all around them Oak Cliff looked like a war zone with battered buildings and loss of life, inside the little bungalow at 202 S. Montreal, all thankfully were alive and well.

Butterbeans with Ham

1 pound fresh butterbeans
1/2 cup bacon drippings
1 cup green bell peppers, chopped
1 cup onions, chopped
1 cup celery, chopped
3 teaspoons garlic powder
1/2 pound cooked ham, cubed
2 ham hocks
1 cup green onions, chopped
1/2 cup fresh parsley, chopped
salt and pepper to taste

Rinse and sort beans. In the refrigerator soak them overnight in cold water. When they are ready to cook, rinse beans once again in cold water. In a large pot melt bacon drippings. Add bell peppers, onions, and celery. Sauté until vegetables are tender. Add garlic, ham, and ham hocks and cook 5 additional minutes. Add butterbeans and enough cold water to cover beans about 2 inches. Add green onions; bring to a rolling boil. Reduce to simmer and allow to cook 30 minutes. Stir occasionally to keep vegetables from scorching. Continue to cook about 1 hour until beans are tender. Stir occasionally. Season to taste with salt and pepper. With a stirring spoon mash about 1/4 of the beans against the side of the pot until they are creamy in nature. Garnish with parsley. Be sure the beans are tender before you serve them. Serves 6-8.

Chapter 9

Little Dusty and the Missing Wedding Dress

In the same way many new brides feel about their parents, I could hardly wait until I could host my mom and dad for their first meal with us in our new home. For this to occur after Louis and I wed in 1969 was a bit more complicated than for many couples, since my parents lived in Garland and the two of us had begun married life in Louisville, KY, where my husband attended seminary.

Nevertheless, some nine months after our wedding Mother and Daddy packed up their car and motored over to the Bluegrass State so they could view their only child in her faraway, married environment. I now realize that my daddy spent most of their visit in much pain, since he underwent prostate surgery as soon as he arrived back in Texas. But he put on his best game face so he and Mother could rest confident I was doing well in my New Kentucky Home.

My menu entree for that first supper on my Antique Grape wedding pottery and new Oneida flatware was a Pork and Lima Skillet (see page 75). Naturally my parents effused with compliments. The next day our agenda included trips to the State Capitol in Frankfort, past horse farms in Lexington, and to the Claudia Sanders Inn, the original restaurant run by "the Colonel."

But the place they most wanted to see was Churchill Downs, with more than just a passing interest in this Louisville landmark. On that legendary spot, just before their visit, their very daughter had made something of an entry into racing record-book history. By an amazing blitz of luck I had just become the first female reporter ever admitted to the previously all-male press box for the Kentucky Derby.

Having majored in journalism in college, my "putting-hubby-through" job while Louis studied for the ministry was working as a reporter in the Louisville bureau of United Press International wire service. Though I'd never set foot on a track (women reporters "didn't" in those days), my boss, Bob Weston, often had me rewrite the male reporters' stories about local races in this horse-crazed state.

History intervened in 1970 when the field of 17 horses entering the 96th Kentucky Derby drew a unique contestant—a rising female jockey named Diane Crump. Realizing that Diane—the first female Derby entrant ever—might accidentally win the Run for the Roses, my boss got a press badge for me. He feared no male reporters could gain a dressing-room interview.

At the same time, he got an additional badge for Louis, to "protect" me in case some of the hard-bitten sports writers in the press box got out of hand. Hardly believing this turn of events, we were off to the races. To make sure I looked the part in this auspicious moment, I wore a large, floppy-brimmed navy hat to accessorize my pink dress with its navy trimmed, box-pleat skirt.

To say that the cigar-smoking, julep-sipping male press contingent in this good-ole-boy bastion high atop Churchill Downs was shocked as a female co-laborer tripped in was a massive understatement. Trying to act nonplussed I pushed through the cigar smoke, sidled up to the rail overlooking the track, and silently pulled for Diane so she and I both could get our moments in the sun. Louis wondered what his seminary colleagues would think if they could see us in such a non-ecclesiastical setting.

Though the 96th running of the Kentucky Derby that afternoon was rife with surprises, a victory by the female rider atop her mount, Fathom, was not one of them. Thoroughbreds Silent Screen and My Dad George were highly favored. Throughout much of the race, one of them seemed sure to win.

But in the homestretch under the twin spires, a nobody horse named Dust Commander began sliding by other opponents. As the fans' collective jaws dropped, jockey Mike Manganello pressed the small chestnut stallion on determinedly. My UPI boss, at my right, was incredulous. "It's Dust Commander! It's Dust Commander!" he howled as little Dusty flew unchallenged under the finish wire. Even today I can hear Bob bellow as this true "darkhorse" won the Derby shocker by five lengths.

Though she finished 15th in the race and did not win, place, or show, Diane Crump did consent to post-race interviews to discuss her history-making run in the first jewel of racing's Triple Crown. My navy floppy-brimmed hat and I were conspicuously there front-and-center; by an hour later my story was filed on the national newswire. In all the years hence, 5:04 p.m. on the first Saturday in May is almost a hallowed moment around our house. Whatever we're doing stops as Louis and I join the televised crowd to warble "My Old Kentucky Home" just before, "And they're off!" is heard.

Now, when I view female racing commentators and reporters dotting the Derby landscape—sometimes even outnumbering the men—I always marvel as I remember: I got to be there first.

* * * * * * * *

An even more memorable dinner than that first one in Kentucky occurred the time my parents traveled to visit Louis and me in our new townhome in Houston in 1972.

I wanted to be sure everything was shipshape in this, our first dwelling to ever own, so I had taken to the cleaners the blue-and-aqua-flowered spread from our kingsized bed. My mother accompanied me as I picked up the spread just after they drove in from Garland.

As I stepped to the counter to pay for my item, I happened to glance over the clerk's shoulder to spot a familiar, startling sight. Dangling from a wire hanger and swaying in the breeze in the middle of the cleaners' steamy back room was a gown that looked suspiciously like my own wedding dress!

About two months earlier I had brought my budget-buster wedding dress to this very establishment to have it cleaned, preserved, and boxed. I had paid almost $100 to have it "heirloomed" and packed away for posterity. In its fancy, gold-foiled container, it now reposed on a shelf in my closet. Could another customer have brought in a gown identical to mine? *How coincidental*, I thought. Distracted from making payment, I asked the clerk to let me have a closer look.

"Does that gown belong to some customer?" I inquired.

"Probably, but we don't know who," the clerk shrugged. "It's been hanging here for a while. Maybe someone will recognize it and claim it."

I fingered the collar of reembroidered lace on the silk-organza and Alencon-lace gown she brought forth. *No doubt about it*, I thought. *My dress, all right. But if my gown were here*—swinging in the breeze of a dank cleaners backroom— *then what was in the box I had brought home from the dry cleaners weeks ago?*

Still in disbelief, my mother and I raced home, where I split upstairs to the shelf on which the supposed "heirloomed" gown in its large gold box lay. Naturally I had never opened it; that would have exposed it to air and could undo the sanitizing. But now I threw out caution, ripped through the packaging, and lifted the lid to reveal—*NOTHING but profuse bunches of wadded-up tissue paper that made the box heavy and gave the impression of something inside!* Furious, I sped back to the cleaners with my empty box to demand some answers to this disturbing dilemma. The cleaners groveled and begged me to let it try again to preserve my dress and make things right. I declined. I didn't want to entrust my wedding gown to these con artists any longer.

What would have happened if I hadn't gone back in to pay for my bedspread? I thought in horror. I knew that only on a cold day in August would I ever have the nerve to leave my gown at any cleaners again.

As years went by, my wedding dress lay merely enfolded in a muslin sheet under my bed. It moved with us during all our relocations but because of my fears was never properly packaged away. My daughter, Katie, played "bride" in it and envisioned herself wearing another (certainly not Mom's outdated one!) wedding dress one day. We took photos of her modeling it and then folded it back up in the faithful sheet. I never let it far from my sight.

Only two years after Katie ultimately *was* a bride and we had her splendid, Priscilla of Boston wedding gown heirloomed at an upscale North Dallas specialty cleaners (where they photographed the gown as they lay it in the box and put a cellophane viewing window on the box lid) did I regain trust in a dry-cleaners again.

In honor of our 40th wedding anniversary I haltingly deigned to take my dress in and have this same company put it away as I had done with Katie's. The specialty cleaners took three months and $500 worth of work to get it back in shape, but I wasn't sorry. A once-burned customer takes a long, long time to rehabilitate.

As to what I served my parents that night as we sat in a stupor over the Missing Wedding-Dress saga, I remember only the Sunshine Gelatin Salad (page 158), with its colorful carrots, pineapple, and cheese enfolded in lemon gelatin.

At least something furnished us a ray of sunshine while the dry-cleaners incident still lay churning in all of our minds.

Pork and Lima Skillet

3 1/2 cups fresh (or 2 10-ounce packages frozen)
   lima beans
5 or 6 smoked pork loin chops
1 teaspoon chicken-flavored gravy base
1 tablespoon all-purpose flour
1/2 teaspoon dried basil, crushed
3/4 cup water

Cook limas in boiling water until tender. If using frozen limas cook according to package directions. Omit salt in cooking water; drain. In skillet brown chops over medium heat. Remove chops from skillet. Pour off all but 1 tablespoon drippings. Add gravy base to skillet. Blend in flour and basil. Add 3/4 cup water; cook and stir over medium heat till thickened and bubbly. Add limas to skillet; stir to coat with sauce. Arrange chops over limas. Cover and cook over low heat about 5 minutes or until heated through. Serves 5 or 6.

Chapter 10

Pumpkin Anything

I was bent over painting a wooden rocker on the grass outside the back porch of our family farmhouse in Round Top. As I looked up to admire the full moon that helped light my nighttime work area, I spotted something that resembled a small, oncoming armored car on four squat legs. This object, with its glaring, manic eyes that looked like something out of an Alfred Hitchcock movie, was charging right in my direction!

"Help!" I shrieked, loud enough to be heard to the next county. Louis appeared at the door with our children, Matthew and Katie, on his coattails. "A crazed armadillo is running right toward me!" I hollered and sprinted to the porch.

Naturally, by that point the armadillo had halted to a slow amble several feet away from where I had painted. Louis saw nothing particularly amiss; nevertheless he galloped back inside to get his 22-caliber rifle, which he kept on hand to frighten off critters, and emerged again.

"*Bam!*" blasted the 22. Louis, with no idea whether he'd actually hit his mark, watched the grizzled armadillo clunk dully off to the side.

No one in my family really ever seemed to believe my tale that an armadillo, a species known for its slow, plodding ways, had been barreling after me in hot pursuit.

However, no one had any trouble believing that the armadillo had sought shelter under our farmhouse. The odiferous remains of his carcass as he perished under the flooring stayed with us for many weeks later.

* * * * * * * *

My encounter with the lunatic armadillo represented one of the hundreds of bonding experiences that our family members shared during our children's growing-up days at the little yellow farmhouse, our weekend home in the foothills of Texas' Guadalupe Mountains.

The historic Round Top area, about an hour-and-a-half's drive from our full-time residence, was a popular spot for Houstonians to own country property. Its gently rolling, rural terrain was a profusion of wildflowers in spring and provided a relatively close-by escape from big-city life.

For me and Louis, who by then co-labored under the same roof as *Houston Chronicle* reporters, disengaging from work pressures so we could have a calm family life was difficult at best.

Loading up our car and heading west with the kids on Friday afternoons was an enforced, weekly break that brought an inestimable lowering of our blood-pressures. On the wall of our rural home hung a cross-stitched sign, "No Chronicle spoken here." Shop-talk was forbidden, even when we entertained top Chronicle executives there. Our "KLMK Farm" (its acronym formed from the initials of our four first names) was off-limits to any discussion that did not concern fun, family, or fixing up our cottage.

Besides, the KLMK gave us a locus to acquaint our kids with the kind of country idyll that Louis and I had known during our respective summers with farm kin when we grew up. Memories of summers at Aunt Bonnie and Uncle Bill's for me and Aunt Tennie and Uncle W.C.'s for Louis were never far away from us once we rolled onto our gravel driveway and past the white picket fence and the peach-tree rows.

I wanted our kids to wake up on country-bright Saturday

mornings to the smell of bacon frying and to monster slabs of French toast that just seemed to taste better when eaten in the clean, rural air. I wanted them to take carefree, extravagant walks in the pasture and to look at clear, star-spattered skies away from city lights.

* * * * * * * *

Our sunshine-colored house with its white trim and L-shaped front porch was a story in itself. Years before it had been situated on a lot in town, but a previous owner had decided to move the structure to a five-acre plot a few miles away down a rural road. The house had been transported in two sections.

When the transport truck arrived with the two segments, the owners had them positioned about 14-feet further apart from each other than they had been before. Carpenters connected the two halves and thus created additional square-footage for the bungalow. The spacious front portion—originally a tiny entry hall—that had been formed from the restructuring expanded into a large dining room for us. Family members traveled from Oklahoma, Cooper, Dallas, and other locales to attend our Thanksgiving dinners there. The KLMK was a ready draw for Houston friends who enjoyed moseying over to Round Top for a pleasant drive in the country.

On our picturesque tract, which had been part of Stephen F. Austin's original land grant when Texas was a republic, we installed a stocked pond, where our kids learned to fish and to drift in an inflatable boat.

Louis bought a pair of registered Polled Herefords, to be named Victory and Smurfette, so our kids could experience growing up around farm animals. Much stir was created in our rural area when Victory birthed twin bulls, whom Matthew named Victor and Vincent. Louis began seeing dollar signs when he thought about how much profit he might make from breeding these identical Hereford males.

The laugh was on him when the vet told him twin bulls are always sterile. The cows he thought would be much-sought-after actually had no value for their reproductive capacity!

In a garden tract out back Louis planted pumpkin seeds. We hoped we were lucky enough to grow just one for a Halloween jack-o-lantern.

Instead, bodacious pumpkins popped out on vine after vine. What to do with such an abundant, ubiquitous crop? Louis helped me scour cookbooks for recipes. Ann Criswell, the *Chronicle*'s food editor whose work cubicle adjoined mine, joined in with pumpkin recipe suggestions.

That year, Christmas gifts for family and friends were no-brainers: jars of Pumpkin Butter, made from our yield. We also enjoyed trying Pumpkin-Pecan Pie, Pumpkin Bread Pudding, Pumpkin Pancakes, and Pumpkin Pound Cake . . . pumpkin anything . . . all thanks to our little plot of ground at Round Top that we tended only on weekends.

* * * * * * *

Not all farm memories were halcyon and picture-perfect. One summer day at lunchtime Matthew and Katie dashed out to our SUV to retrieve some audiotapes so they could play music while we dined.

Some time later we began calling for our poodle, Klifford, a little white creampuff who had been a birthday present for Matthew. We found no sign of our fluffy, spoiled-silly puppy. We called and called again. We searched in closets, in the pantry, under the porch, and any place he might have "escaped" in the past. We divided up to scour the pasture and to run down the lane to the county road.

Finally someone thought of looking in the SUV, which was not parked under the shade tree as usual but sat unprotected in the unrelenting noontime Texas sun. There, in the back end, was sprawled out Klifford—deader than mackerel. Unknown to them he apparently had trailed our kids out to the car and remained behind after they found their tapes and returned inside. With no windows lowered in the vehicle, the inescapable heat claimed him quickly.

We yanked up his lifeless body and rushed him to the house, where we laid him out on the cool floor under the air-conditioner.

In a grief-racked, desperate voice I phoned the vet in near-by LaGrange. The sympathetic doctor offered to drive out to our rural location if we wanted him to but advised us that, based on what we described, he could do nothing. Klifford indeed had expired.

All four of us blubbered like babies. Adults and children alike, we blamed ourselves. If only we had observed Kliffy leaving the house . . . if only the kids had looked behind when they left the car with the tapes . . . if only we hadn't waited so long to discover him missing . . .. The hapless self-flagellation was terrible. An adorable little white puppy just hours ago had been happily frisking at his kids' heels; now those soulful, brown pool eyes of his were closed forever.

Then we pondered what to do with his remains—whether to carry him home to bury him in our back yard or to lay him to rest at the farm, where he loved to frolic. We knew that by the time we could get packed up, on the road, and back to our Houston home, his stiff, pathetic body would look even more heartbreaking than it did now. Louis began digging a resting place for him under the big shade tree up by the farmhouse.

Our grief spilled over to our animal-loving neighbors, the Harpers, who knew how nuts we all were about Klifford. They offered to stand alongside us under the shade tree while we put him under. The very embodiments of compassion, the Harpers brought us some blue artificial flowers, which we stuck in the ground after the dirt closed in over him, and ached with us at the loss of a beloved pet.

Tears continued to flow unheeded on our way back to Houston until Louis had the good instinct to stop in a Dairy Queen in Sealy. He bought us all candy-laced, soft-serve ice cream to make us feel better. Something about the insanely cold confection seemed to wipe out all ills.

Some weeks later a new, endearing little gray poodle named Pepper arrived to fill the empty spot in our home. Naturally we ferried him with us to the KLMK Farm. But like obsessively overprotective parents the four of us hardly ever let him out of our sights.

* * * * * * *

Ultimately our family relocated from Houston to Plano. We still made periodic trips to the farm, but travel to Round Top required almost four hours now instead of the simpler 1 1/2. We missed the weekend escape place but still tried to get there for holidays, especially Thanksgiving. Without the ability to check up on it regularly, growing pumpkins with abandon as we had in earlier years became impossible. Gradually we were weaning ourselves away from the spot that once had been such a wellspring of joy.

When Louis accepted a new job in Nashville and we began our Eastward migration that would rip us away from Texas for the next 11 years, holding on to the Round Top property no longer was possible or practical. A "For Sale" sign went up on the sunshine-colored farmhouse with the L-shaped front porch and the white picket fence all around.

As far as we know, Klifford still rests under the big shade tree near where the wild-eyed, hard-charging armadillo scared me senseless. But whenever we dine on Pumpkin Butter, Pumpkin Pancakes, Pumpkin-Pecan Pie, Pumpkin Bread Pudding . . . pumpkin anything . . . piquant memories surface—of the garden and food and the laughter and the fun.

Pumpkin-Pecan Pie

2 eggs
1/4 cup sugar
1/4 cup brown sugar, packed
1 teaspoon all-purpose flour
1 teaspoon pumpkin pie spice
1/4 teaspoon salt
2/3 cup cooked pumpkin, mashed and drained
2/3 cup milk
1 (9-inch) unbaked deep-dish pastry shell

Pecan Topping:
2 eggs
1/2 cup dark corn syrup
2 tablespoons brown sugar
2 tablespoons molasses
1 tablespoon all-purpose flour
1 teaspoon vanilla extract
1/2 teaspoon salt
1/2 cup chopped pecans
1 cup pecan halves

In a mixing bowl beat eggs, sugars, flour, pie spice and salt until smooth. Mix in mashed and drained pumpkin. Gradually beat in milk. Pour into pastry shell. Bake at 425 degrees for 10 minutes. Reduce the temperature to 350 degrees and bake 15 minutes longer. For pecan topping beat eggs in a mixing bowl until foamy. Add corn syrup, brown sugar, molasses, flour, vanilla, and salt. Pour over filling. Sprinkle with chopped pecans; cover with pecan halves. Continue baking at 350 degrees for 30-35 minutes or until set. Cool completely. Store in the refrigerator. Makes 6-8 servings.

Chapter 11
No Room at the Inn

Way up there with celebrating Christmas itself was a very weird, other crown-jewel moment of the holiday season. For me the act of packing for our annual Christmas trip brought a high that was practically equal to frosting cutout cookies and hearing our church choir sing Handel's *Messiah*.

Something about washing and pressing and folding our Christmas clothes for the suitcase—all the while imagining what fun we'd soon have as we wore them for the events ahead—always gave me an amazing rush.

I savored the heavy air of expectancy that reigned with festive gifts at last lining our car's rear windows, luggage crowding the overflowing trunk; and Louis, Matthew, Katie and I pulling out of the driveway to head "over the river and through the woods" to Grandma's house for another Christmas.

So what, I reasoned, if the children's behavior was less than Currier-and-Ives like and the trip dragged us over more than 700 miles of highway from our new location in Nashville? We were snug, we were together, and we were headed for some good family times. I could hardly wait to pull out some of our favorite travel games such as "Find Somebody Who" and to chorus along with tapes such as "Wee Sing Songs for Christmas."

Part of our anticipation, I'm sure, had to do with imagining the Christmas feast we would enjoy at Yvonne and Joe's house on Christmas Day. As the generations flowed on, the task of hosting the family holiday dinner passed from Aunt Bonnie, who had faithfully welcomed us each year during Christmases of my childhood, to her daughter, who with Joe lived in town in Cooper.

Yvonne, with the Miller Girls' penchant for industry, creativity, and precision, made preparing a monster meal seem effortless. Part of this was her skill in preparing her home-grown vegetables, the thought of which set me salivating as I passed all those car miles from Tennessee back to Texas.

During the summers a man who lived about one-half mile from the Cooper Dairy Queen, out the road to Antioch in west Delta County, let Joe garden on a tract of land on his property. Joe's garden spot was about the size of an average front yard. Sweet potatoes, green beans, tomatoes, cantaloupe, and blackberries from the man's established vines were plenteous under Joe's cultivation.

One summer Joe and Yvonne, now retired, went to Eureka Springs on vacation and left my cousin Bill in charge of the garden. During their absence the cantaloupe crop came in. "We must have had 100 cantaloupes," Bill recalled later. "I gave them away to anyone who would take them."

After the owner of Joe's borrowed garden spot moved from the area, Joe took over a garden tract when Bill and his wife, Jana, bought some land on which they would ultimately build a house, just across the cul de sac from where Joe and Yvonne lived. The agreement was that Bill would till the soil; Joe would follow behind with his plantings.

"He told me he would set out some tomato plants, and I said fine," Bill remembers. "I arrived to find that he had put in 38 tomato plants" that yielded enough tomatoes that could have fed all of Delta County.

Joe and Yvonne's grandkids—Bill and Jana's Shelley and Jason, Lynda's Jarod and Brett, and Mark and Eleene's Marleene—often were drafted as assistant gardeners when they visited PawPaw and MeMaw at one of these two garden projects in Cooper.

Yvonne seemingly could toss a little kitchen pixie dust over food and steaming dishes of vegetables and delectable fruits, all seasoned to perfection and brimming with freshness, would appear in a dazzling array of sides. No wonder I often got distracted in rhapsodic, pre-Christmas euphoria as our loaded car headed west for the 12-hour trip to Texas.

Distraction became a problem, however, when it sidetracked us from listening to the weather report before our car backed out of the driveway on this particular Christmas adventure in December 1991.

We were most surprised when a profusion of ice flecks began to pellet our windshield just before we arrived in Jackson, TN, only a few hours into our trip.

* * * * * * * *

In those days Caesar Augustus issued a decree that a census should be taken of the entire Roman world . . . And everyone went to his own town to register (Luke 2:1, 3).

Earlier that day, all had seemed well. Dry roads, temperatures in the 20s, an occasional snowflake, but not even enough to excite Katie and Matthew. We were having a rollicking time as we munched the caramel corn I had fixed just for our trip.

No sooner had the first ice flecks descended than the roads turned ominous. First they appeared as small patches of ice, then huge, icy sheets that left only tiny specks of concrete peeping through. By then the snow was pouring down, but no shrieks of delight emerged from the children's lips. They—all of us—could see we were in trouble. Traffic backed up and crawled. A seven-mile stretch of road construction that normally would have been a mere inconvenience virtually locked our car into one spot for two hours.

"Mommy, read to me," begged a bored, 9-year-old Katie.

"Honey, I can't. We need to help Daddy," I warned. The string of brown concrete patches that now represented a lifeline to keep our car from sliding off the road showed up less often now. All four pairs of our eyes were needed to help Louis negotiate what had become a frightening blizzard.

While they were there, the time came for the baby to be born . . . (Luke 2:6).

"If we can just make it to Little Rock," my husband murmured, with the hope a major city would yield better roads—and better weather. Wrong! Little Rock was buried under ice and teen temps. By now we had been driving on almost solid ice for hours; dark was falling. We contemplated stopping at a motel, but thoughts of reaching my parents' home, with their usual welcoming hearth fire and hot cocoa, caused us to push on. Bad decision. More ice. More blinding snow. Now cars in ditches every few feet—cars in 360-degree spins on every side.

Just when matters seemed beyond getting worse or more scary, traffic reached a total standstill. A man two cars ahead with a CB radio (in days before cell phones and hand-held weather updates) emerged to inform other drivers that two 18-wheelers had jackknifed and blocked the road. Bumper to bumper, we sat for three hours. As far as we could see, cars ahead of us had turned off engines and lights and prepared possibly for an all-night wait. Bundled in coats, gloves, and mufflers, we envisioned spending the night huddled and parked on the frozen road—with the nearby snow-covered woods for our bathroom.

Hopes rose again when the snarl cleared and we managed

to inch our way to the next town—Arkadelphia, AR. Now at midnight, we had been traveling 16 hours. When we spotted a Holiday Inn marquee on the horizon, we cheered, but one look at the parking lot assured us it was beyond full. What a disaster my eagerly awaited car trip had turned into! *Surely this will go down as our worst Christmas ever*, I thought angrily. Didn't my family deserve something more, well, Currier-and-Ives than this?

* * * * * * * *

Nothing could have prepared us for the scene we witnessed after we pulled into the lot and made our way to the motel's registration desk. Several hundred people, forced in by the weather, were jammed onto sofas, chairs, and into telephone booths—anything that could be a makeshift bed for a few hours.

"We've been out of rooms since 4 o'clock. Churches and Red Cross shelters in town are full as well," a sympathetic but harried motel clerk told my husband. "You're welcome to stay indoors here until the weather clears. Maybe you can find some spots back in the corner of the dining room." We tiptoed over the wall-to-wall sleeping mass that resembled scenes after Hurricane Katrina and prepared to stay the night—somehow, someway.

The motel earlier had run out of extra blankets and sheets, so we improvised a pallet for Matthew and Katie by stretching our four coats side by side, while Louis and I lined up four metal dining-table chairs for beds. For cover Louis scoured the darkened motel kitchen until he found a supply of tablecloths, which we gratefully threw over the kids and us—not warm by any means but certainly serviceable to keep off drafts.

As I at last stretched out on my makeshift bed, I realized the scene had an unmistakably familiar ring.

. . . and she gave birth to her firstborn, a son. She wrapped him in cloths and placed him in a manger, because there was no room for them in the inn (Luke 2:7).

Another family, in another time, had undertaken a journey with a seemingly disappointing ending. Didn't God's Son deserve a better birthplace than in a dinner room for cattle? Yet, when the inn's rooms were full, the mother and earthly father that God chose for a special task improvised resourcefully—the way we had just done for our family. They found a stable corner for lodging, a feeding tray for a cradle, and likely hay for a mattress. They were safe—they were together. This Christmas journey had the most miraculous ending of all.

My anger and frustration turned to peace. God was allowing us to walk through Bethlehem with Mary and Joseph! God certainly doesn't will people to be trapped in ice storms, but He sometimes uses our calamities as windows into a greater truth. In the middle of this cramped motel dining room God was helping the Christmas story leap off the Bible's pages and into contemporary experience. Was I being reminded, perhaps, that Christmas was more than an idyllic, well-orchestrated car trip? In our hardship, as we identified with that inconvenienced earthly family of Jesus, had we stumbled onto the most delectable Christmas moment of all?

I drifted into a short and cramped but welcomed sleep. The time was 1 a.m. on Christmas Eve; a new day was but a few hours over the horizon. We could still be home in time for Christmas. I could still salivate over Yvonne's garden-fresh dishes (see Cinnamon Apples, page 91) which awaited on Christmas Day. Now I would have a new/old Christmas story to tell our family in the car on the last stretch of our journey. This just might be our best Christmas ever!

Cinnamon Apples

1 cup sugar
4 to 5 large baking apples
1/2 cup red-hot cinnamon candies

On the stove over medium heat cook apples in small amount of water until soft. Add cinnamon candies that have been melted in 1/2 cup water in microwave. Add sugar and cook until most of the liquid is gone. Red food color can be added, if desired. Serves 8-10.

Chapter 12
Peach Trees and the Wedding Plywood

Do we all need to start building an ark?
That was the question on everyone's minds during the spring of 2007, when downpours of biblical proportions occurred in our area of Texas.

For endless days during May, rain clouds formed. Mornings, afternoons, evenings, overnight—the gullywashers went on.

This was wonderful news for gardeners but terrifying for people planning an outdoor wedding reception.

We were among the latter.

From her girlhood Katie yearned to have part of her wedding occur in her Grandma Wheeler's backyard garden. Every spring Grandma's yard—once the fruit orchard and vegetable garden of the Hunt family next door—was resplendent with iris, peonies, daylilies, begonias, impatiens, azaleas, and other rapturous bursts of color.

When my mother died and we leased out her home, in the rental contract Louis specified that the tenants would give us access to their back yard at 412 South 11th Street if we ever desired to conduct a wedding reception there.

Now we so desired. Katie wanted everything to occur under a massive white tent, with fine china, a string quartet, and flowers galore.

Check. This we can do.

The caterer was hired, the menu selected, the tent people called, the quartet auditioned, the centerpieces arranged, the place cards and favors all made by hand. The tables were set up around Granddaddy Wheeler's giant pecan tree all twined with twinkle lights. The buffet spread was designed with Grandma's birdbath as its focal piece.

Everything was perfectly in order—everything except the weather, which as any schoolchild knows, is totally out of human hands. God alone is in charge of the elements. He is sovereign.

* * * * * * *

God's sovereignty was never more evident than in the happenings that led Katie to find her life's mate—the event that put all these wedding plans into motion.

After getting her Baylor degree in Spanish, Katie enrolled at Southwestern Seminary in Fort Worth to become a Christian counselor. From her little bungalow on Fort Worth's far west side she began visiting singles programs at churches in the area. None of them seemed a good fit. Meanwhile, she began having second thoughts about her career choice. Profoundly gifted in Spanish, she missed her pursuit of languages. She transferred to Dallas Baptist University and finished her master's hours but did not feel led to take the counseling study further. She returned to her first love by enrolling in the doctoral program in linguistics at the University of Texas at Arlington.

With the transfer to DBU, Katie also moved her locus to our side of the Dallas/Fort Worth Metroplex. To our surprise she rented a house only about six blocks from where we lived in Garland. Singles programs in Dallas-area churches now became an option. She began attending the Mesquite campus of LakePointe Church, a megachurch based in Rockwall. The singles class there blossomed at first but then withered. Katie was unsure where to turn next.

At the Southern Baptist Convention in 2004 a pastor friend and his wife remarked to Louis and me that their son taught a singles class at LakePointe's main campus in Rockwall. They suggested that Katie look him up. Though the church was behemoth, the singles class made her feel special. Later, Renée, Katie's college roommate and now housemate in Garland, joined her at LakePointe in Rockwall. Katie finally believed she had found a post-college congregation that was a keeper.

One Sunday morning she noted two new faces in the class—two young men who had traveled down I-30 from Greenville, since singles ministries in their smaller town were limited.

After hearing one of the guys—the red-haired one—discuss Scripture impressively during the Bible study, she surmised he must be a seminary student. Gregarious though she was, Katie did not learn many particulars on either of the two new guests that day.

The red-haired one, however, made a point of digging up the particulars on Katie. After he and his friend left the class, he remarked, "It's the blue-eyed one on the front row." Not long afterward, he learned her name: Katie Moore.

Katie messed up big-time in her assessment. The impressive visitor who spoke up in class wasn't a seminary student as her parents always thought she might marry but was an engineer in Greenville at the same company where Katie's cousin Bill happened to work.

The visitor, however, was right on the money about Katie. It *was* the blue-eyed one on the front row. A year later, on September 14, he became our future son-in-law—Casey Welch, a godly guy who happened to know a lot about the Bible because he had read it—and followed it—all his life.

What better dream man could parents want for their daughter's Prince Charming? Besides, he would be the first redhead to join the family since Mable was born 95 years earlier. *Wahoo!*

* * * * * * * *

Our contingency plan for the reception was simple: in case of rain, close down the side walls of the tent. The party continues without a hitch. Guests are transported from the church in a bus; umbrellas are stationed at the garden gate.

Let it rain! we exulted. Nothing would rain on our parade.

And nothing *would* have, if the rain had fallen like gentle, normal, garden-variety rain—the kind that occurs in most showers—even in many torrents. The tent had been set up on the site since Thursday before Saturday's nuptials, so the ground underneath would remain nice and dry regardless.

However, this rain rained *sideways*—the only factor on which we had not counted. All day Friday fierce rain pelted *parallel* to the ground and easily be-sopped the dry area under the big top. By Friday evening, when we visited the reception site on our way to Katie and Casey's rehearsal dinner, the ground under the tent was unnavigable.

"Dad, we can't let this ruin Katie's wedding," pled Matthew, whose own wedding to Marcie in Arizona six years earlier had been storybook. "We've gotta do something."

They had fewer than 24 hours to prevent a wedding spoiler in the making.

Louis hardly remembers eating a bite of the delicious rehearsal-dinner barbecue. He spent the entire time on the phone in a panicked conversation alternating among the tent people, Home Depot, and Lowe's. By dinner's end he had a plan, but it wasn't pretty. He and Matthew would begin at 6 a.m. the next morning hauling any available piece of floor-grade plywood in Garland to cover over the 4,000-square-foot reception site. That meant removing all tables and 250 chairs already in place, installing a subflooring, stretching out the plywood, and laying artificial grass on top. An already busy day just grew maddening. Before daybreak on Saturday Louis and Matthew hit the streets in a frantic race against time.

* * * * * * *

Katie's garden wedding reception wasn't the first such event to be held on Garland's historic 11th Street. Almost from childhood I had heard about the fine, long-ago weddings of the Tucker girls in a beautiful garden adjoining their home, one of the oldest on the street and situated two blocks north of my parents' residence at 412. The Tucker girls, in the early part of the last century, married men who went on to be prominent Garlandites. One of the Tucker brides was Dixie Crossman, our neighbor two houses down. I easily could imagine Mrs. Crossman, ever elegant as she tossed many a Garland social "do", standing under a vine-covered trellis to greet her groom, also a member of a storied Garland family. For hours Margaret Branham, whose home ultimately stood over the old Tucker gardens, would entertain me with tales of our 11th Street when it was Garland's "silk-stocking district" in the olden days.
    Katie would pass under a vine-covered trellis, also—her grandma's wisteria-laden arbor now spun with twinkle lights. But would she step into a sea of water-sogged St. Augustine?
    Louis and Matthew and some workers helping us in this emergency would be the ones to save the day, if it could be saved at all.

* * * * * * * *

Throughout Wedding Day, we saw neither hide nor hair of Louis—infrequent cell-phone blasts kept me up with his progress, which didn't sound promising as the 5 p.m. wedding time approached. At 3 p.m. our family needed to depart for the church. Where was Louis and our family vehicle? He and Matthew had left it in a Lowe's lot and rented a flat-bed to carry the plywood from the store to the tent site. At 3:05, when I finally was able to move Katie's dress, my dress, and other wedding apparatii to our truck as it pulled into our driveway, Louis confessed sadly, "I don't think we can get it ready in time."

Later Louis recalled the most difficult thing he had to do all day was not giving away his "Daddy's-girl" in marriage; it was handing the scene of chaos under the tent over to a fragmented, understaffed crew who at 3 p.m. still struggled to install the subflooring before the plywood could be set down. But turn it over he must, because no one but he could be Father of the Bride.

Realizing someone else would have to finish the task, he left it in God's hands.

* * * * * * * *

The church filled up with guests, many of whom RSVP'ed "yes" just so they could catch a glimpse of their beloved Mable's yard duded up for a party.

As I watched devoted friends and loved ones file in, I shuddered with dread that they might be treated to a dud of a reception.

However, they certainly would get their money's worth out

of Katie and Casey's splendid ceremony. A choir perched in the balcony sang *a cappella* as she and Casey knelt at the altar. Stradivarius strings wafted bridesmaids down the aisle on a bold Pachelbel *Canon*. Katie's colossal veil gleaming with Swarovski crystals gave her a "Princess Di" moment as it fanned out dramatically on the steps up to their kneeling bench. A Latin choral number hand-picked by Casey—the groom!—piped out for the couple's exit. A mighty organ postlude—remembered from Matthew's college graduation recessional and saved in my "wedding file"—boomed forth as the audience poured out.

Magnifique!

But would the reception put us to shame? Thunder pealed just as the ceremony started. Moist sidewalks told me we'd had another shower while the wedding was under way. *What was happening at the tent site?* By the time Louis and I broke free from post-wedding photos, we knew guests already had reached the backyard dining area. Katie and Casey's ceremony had lasted a full hour, but had that given the crew enough time to finish the task?

As I inched toward the garden hedge, with Louis' hand steadying me lest I faint from fright, I squeezed my eyes shut.

Then I heard . . . strings music playing joyfully in the background.

Glasses and silverware clinking.

Lilting conversation.

I opened my eyes a tad. Candles flickered in the distance.

Centerpieces were in place.

Seated guests filled themselves as sumptuous appetizers were passed.

Tiki torches glowed around my dad's pecan tree.

I looked at the group assembled. People from all arenas of my life . . . childhood friends . . . former teachers . . . kinfolks

. . . Katie's professors . . . Casey's neighbors—all dining happily on toothsome hors d'oeuvres.

Had I been transported to heaven? Surely this was a glimpse of what heaven would be like, as we feast in glad reunion at the luxuriant banquet of the Bridegroom.

No, but I *had* witnessed a modern-day miracle. Somehow, some way, while the kids were marrying, the reception site got pulled together perfectly. *No guest suspects a thing!* I realized. *Thank You, thank You, God! You certainly showed up today!*

And from the moment the ceremony ended, nary a drop of rain fell the rest of the evening. The clouds moved away as if on cue.

As Katie and Casey rode off in a dazzling blaze of glory—and birdseed—the twinkle-light glow on the garden hedge was matched by the glow of the stars in an absolutely clear night sky.

Surely this gave my mother an unobscured view from the balustrade of heaven as she peered down on this monumental event in her own back yard.

* * * * * * * *

One thing we later learned about the unprecedented rains that fell on us at wedding time—they *had been* bad for gardeners, too.

Not just wedding planners got their hopes dashed. My husband's prized copse of peach trees, so prolific in our own backyard garden—perished from root rot. Too much water zapped them for good. Louis had to plant new baby saplings and launch a peach crop from scratch.

* * * * * * * *

Post-wedding mopup left another big dilemma: what does one do with 150 sheets of plywood, none of which was returnable because it now had nail holes from being attached to the subfloor?

Louis immediately used a small bit of it to double the size of his workshop. A dozen or so more sheets walled in the second floor of our storage barn for my crafts and sewing "garret." A friend purchased another few sheets for a home-improvement project.

But the 120 or so remaining sheets?

I suddenly had a plan. Almost since we were newlyweds Louis had promised me a baby grand piano to replace my upright spinet. Anniversaries sped past. So did birthday milestones. We crept up on 40 years of wedlock. I was about to pass my 60th. No piano. *No room*, Louis would always reply. He was right. Even if I had a baby grand, where would we put the thing?

The *ah-ha* moment arrived when I gazed on the larger-than-life stack of wedding plywood.

A piano room! The plywood can expand the living room behind the fireplace. What a perfect way to keep Katie and Casey's wedding memories alive!

Louis—always practical—warmed to this utilitarian idea, but advisors cautioned: buy the piano first. The room must be built with the exact piano in mind.

We put on our agenda to piano-shop. *At last,* I thought. *My dream may be realized.*

We never had to enter a piano showroom. At the State Fair of Texas, a Dallas music store showed off its wares at the fair's giant exhibit hall. Featured was a small, French-style baby grand of cherry wood. I stumbled into the massive exhibit building, found myself standing right next to this gorgeous instrument, and knew it was for me.

The ultimate State Fair souvenir! It sure beat a monkey on a stick or cotton candy.

Plans were drawn up for the music-room addition—a ceramic-tile floor, walls of floral paper to resemble a conservatory, and a beautiful antique-look fireplace mantle.

Construction took seven long months, but the result was worth the wait. The day my little French baby grand was placed in the center of this beautiful addition, we rejoiced.

Just one thing about it, however: the music room never used a single sheet of wedding plywood. Because the wood was flooring-grade, it was the wrong kind of material the workers needed. Not a single place for it there was ever found.

So even after seven months of construction, the shoulder-high stack of boards remained untouched in a pile outside Louis' workshop!

* * * * * * * *

No peaches grew that first summer on Louis' baby peach trees, nor did they grow the next.

Only three summers later did his trees bud out and form the first peach crop we'd had since the deluge surrounding Katie's wedding.

Deliriously excited I immediately brought in the first batch to make a long-awaited cobbler.

The cobbler was a fitting dessert to be served while wedding bells filled the air again. When my cousin, Lynda, and her fiancé, George Matthews, arrived at our home one June afternoon to discuss their upcoming vows, we all jubilantly dined on the first peach cobbler from the replacement crop.

And the plywood? On their third wedded summer Katie and Casey purchased a large country house with an unfinished attic in which they wanted a game room installed. The plywood at last found its rightful purpose.

Without Katie and Casey we never would have acquired it in the first place.

Quick Peach Cobbler

cinnamon
nutmeg
sugar
4-6 cups sliced and peeled peaches
1 cup self-rising flour
1 cup sugar
1 large egg, beaten
1/2 cup butter
ice cream or whipped topping

Preheat oven to 350 degrees. In a medium bowl place sliced peaches. Sprinkle sugar, cinnamon, and nutmeg on top of sliced peaches. Toss to mix. Place mixture in greased 9-by-9-inch baking dish. Mix 1 cup self-rising flour, 1 cup sugar, and egg to a crumb-like texture. Pour over layer of peaches in baking dish. Melt butter and drizzle over crumb topping. Bake at 350 degrees for 30 minutes or until top turns brown and crusty. Serve hot or cold, plain or with ice cream or whipped topping. Serves 6-8.

Chapter 13
To Love, to Honor, and Surprise

Lynda and George were about to pull off a good one. I could hardly wait to see everyone's faces when the event came down.

Ordinarily I would have been in the dark like most of the others. But Louis, secretly recruited to perform Lynda and George's "surprise" wedding, didn't want to suffer through excruciating weeks while I intuited from him that something was up. He knew I would bug him mercilessly if I so much as glimpsed a flicker of his eyebrow; he knew that pain and wanted no part of it.

Good thing he told me. How else would he have arrived wearing "gerber-daisy colors" like the rest of the wedding party did?

* * * * * * * *

My cousin Lynda, around whom the chapter "The New Cousin" in *Way Back in the Country* revolved, had been a single mom for 16 years now. Everyone had been in awe of how courageously and independently she had reared her two fine boys, Jarod and Brett, as she shouldered the mantle of parenthood and home management alone.

Lynda is such a sweet and deserving person, we all fervently hoped she would find her dream man with whom she could have a bright future as a duo.

As time went on, Lynda met George Matthews, who like

her was rearing two sons from a previous marriage. As with Lynda, George felt responsible for getting his two boys, Grant and Nick, through high school and out on their own before he embarked on any life change.

As George began showing up with Lynda at family gatherings, he fit right in and was much-liked. Personable, a good conversationalist, and clearly smitten with gorgeous Lynda, the two of them, with their golden, All-America features, even looked like each other. Like the proverbial husband and wife who start resembling each other the longer they are wed, Lynda and George became like twins the more they dated. Tanned, blonde, and trim, the two of them made a knockout couple. In contrast to Lynda's vivacity, George was soft-spoken and steady. His appreciation for her was almost palpable. We all wondered when he would pop the question.

Just after Katie and Casey became engaged in 2006, George produced an engagement ring for Lynda. We all exulted. But no wedding date was set; no plans were yet on the table. George's last child was still living at home; Lynda's last-born, Brett, was still in college. Both parents clung to their commitment to put their children first until the time was right.

In 2009 Lynda finally began tossing out a wedding date: the following July, when she and George at last would be fully empty-nested. Plans included an outdoor ceremony at a friend's home. Attendants would be their four children and Cara, Jarod's breathtaking new bride. Lynda loved gerber daisies, so she wanted the men to wear solid polos in orange, gold, and green hues. A friend of George's would perform the ceremony. We all put the July date on our calendars. Wedding bells would ring at last!

Imagine Louis' shock when, one morning, George's voice rang out over Louis' cell phone. Lynda had already planned for the family to gather on June 20 at her house for one of our annual Mesquite barbecue devourings. Would Louis put on his "preacher hat" and preside over their vows right then? The country was in tight times, the planned July outdoor wedding had grown expensive, the family would all be amassed anyway (including some who might not feel able to attend an outdoor event), and he and Lynda had waited long enough.

Louis, honored, composed himself and sputtered a glad "yes". But plans must remain a total and utter secret. Other than the four boys and Cara, absolutely no one was to know!

* * * * * * * *

In pulling a "sneaky" on the family, Lynda had big footprints to follow. A few years before, her very own mother had led the way in switching from announced plans to a quieter, less-heralded wedding ceremony.

Yvonne's loss of Joe to pancreatic cancer in 1999 left the entire town of Cooper—not to mention the family—shaken. No one could imagine Yvonne without her life's mate, regarded by all as the finest man who ever drew a breath. Even when their hair had begun silvering and grandchildren arrived, the two of them still seemed like two young kids in love. During Joe and Yvonne's fairytale wedding, I had been a 1 1/2-year-old sitting in my mother's lap as she quietly read "The Three Bears" to me. Though I have no memory of this event, Joe always was my role model of what a husband should be like; because of him, the bar was always set very high. I can still picture Joe and Yvonne holding hands as they tucked me and my cousin, Mark, into our beds when I spent the night with their family during my summer Cooper visits.

"A man among men" is how one friend of Lynda's later described her daddy 10 years after his passing. Selfless leader,

Sunday-school teacher, pillar of the Cooper community—if Baptists had saints, this man of matchless moral fiber surely would have been one. The line at the funeral home at his viewing wrapped around much of the block as folks poured in to pay tribute. No one could envision how Cooper—much less his dear family—could ever get its equilibrium after Joe's untimely passing.

In widowhood Yvonne busied herself with crafts, church, grandkids, and daily trips to the Dairy Queen for restorative *kaffeeklatches*. Though she wore a brave face and bucked up in the tradition of the stoic, Germanic Millers, seeing her navigate life alone was tough on everyone. She had always been part of a duo.

We saw her travels restricted, since she didn't like to drive alone on the freeways. Doubtless cut from the same genetic cloth as the long-lived Harrises, Yvonne still could have several healthy decades ahead. We knew she needed a companion but couldn't get our minds around someone except Joe by her side. Besides, what person would be brave enough to even think of following such a saint?

* * * * * * * *

Actually, one person was. Early in 2004, on a visit to Dallas to see her two aunts, Yvonne confided over a Saturday meal that she had begun seeing a gentleman friend. Wheat Brooks, a widower whom she had once dated when they were Cooper High School students, had begun calling on her. Early that year his wife, Jean, had died from cancer. Yvonne could sympathize with his loss; she above all people could identify with this crushing sorrow. Ultimately visits began to occur from Wheat, who remembered breathtaking Yvonne and found her still ravishing though in her senior years. At the time Yvonne reported these developments to her aunts Frances and Mable, her two elderly relatives hectored her, "Don't go getting married again, now." Yvonne convincingly assured them she had no such plans—that the two were strictly friends.

Some time later, however, Yvonne spoke with them again—this time to announce her engagement to Wheat. The duo planned a small wedding in the same church where she and Joe had wed 54 years earlier. My cousin, Mark, would be the soloist. Though the spectre of this understandably took some adjustment in both families, we could see Yvonne was sublimely happy—her loneliness abated, her need for companionship filled. We knew that marrying Wheat probably would extend the lives of both of them. We thought Wheat had courage beyond any mere mortal to not only marry Yvonne but to start married life in a place where everyone believed her first husband walked on water. I don't think I've ever envied anyone any less than this man who was determined to win Yvonne's hand.

As we looked toward their nuptials, however, another surprising phone call followed. Wheat and Yvonne had suddenly jettisoned their more expansive plans and instead arranged private vows in the office of Yvonne's pastor. With no family around and no fanfare, they would quietly tie the knot within the next few days. At the last minute a church staffer brought in for them a wedding cake—the lone embellishment at this highly subdued ceremony.

Wheat was considerate, courtly, and a true gentleman—not to mention the luckiest man alive to be Yvonne's new spouse. I admired the way the two of them ardently sought to blend their families to try to make the merger more comfortable for everyone. At Christmas Yvonne worked tirelessly to toss giant holiday bashes to acquaint their respective kids, grands, and great-grands with each other. Louis and I found Wheat's loved ones amiable and interesting to get to know. Lines literally seemed to vanish from Wheat's and Yvonne's faces as the duo settled into a comfortable companionship after each had nursed a spouse through cancer's virulent grip. Wheat was happy to be back living in his former town; he found a group of guys to join for morning coffee.

* * * * * * * *

If anyone seated in Lynda's den for the barbecue suspected they were in a wedding bower, no one let on. While Lynda, who had greeted guests while she wore shorts, slipped upstairs to change, she had Louis assemble the family to purposely stall things in discussing the status of Aunt Frances' probate. Visitors listened politely; a few privately wondered why Louis droned on about this tedious subject.

Then, as matron-of-honor Cara appeared on the stair landing as a cue, Louis suddenly switched gears:

"Folks, we all know that we've waited a long time for Lynda and George to tie the knot. So since the family is all here today, we just thought it would be a good time to go on and get it over with. Is that alright with you, George?"

A beaming George gave a hearty nod. Yvonne's hands went to her mouth. A collective sucking-paint-off-the-walls gasp was heard.

At that moment Lynda, now changed into a flowing ivory crepe gown and escorted by two debonair sons, appeared in the den. Carrying a gerber-daisy bouquet, she and the boys slipped through the group and faced Louis, who now had George and his two precious boys lined up beside him.

* * * * * * * *

A few tears glistened on cheekbones as the reality of the moment soaked in. With her jaw still on the floor, Yvonne, who had just celebrated her five-year anniversary to Wheat, nevertheless grinned through her shock. Her baby girl at last had snagged her man.

The rest of the event was joyous and exactly what Lynda and George said they wanted. In his vows Louis forthrightly addressed the pain of divorce that both families had experienced but emphasized that now was a time for forgiveness, restoration, and a new start. He urged the four boys to support their parents and to endeavor to mesh as a new family unit.

Uncle Herbert's barbecue—joined by some tasty marinated Cucumbers and Onions fresh from Bill's garden—had never been served at such an auspicious occasion. With hugs and good wishes all around, Lynda and George looked relieved and exultant. The long wait was over; the surprise was pulled off masterfully.

The only thing that would have bettered the moment would have been for Lynda's daddy to have been looking on. Perhaps he was. He and George—so much alike in their servant spirits—would have been the best of buddies.

Cucumbers and Onions in Vinegar

2-3 medium cucumbers
1 medium onion
1/2 cup vinegar
1/2 cup water
1 teaspoon salt (optional)
pepper to taste

Peel cucumbers and slice horizontally. Slice onions crosswise. Put cucumbers and onions in bowl. Pour vinegar and water over them. Stir to mix. Chill for several hours before you serve. Serves 6-8.

Chapter 14
Blessed Be the Name of the Lord

One thing can be said of the Red-Haired Miller Girls. None of them went "gentle into that good night."[1] Each fiercely stood death down nose-to-nose.

As a hospice chaplain once explained to me, "This was a generation of survivors. They survived their births during a time of high-infant mortality. They survived early childhood diseases, which took their toll on many. They survived the Great Depression. Survival was part of their DNA."

No wonder, then, that death did not find them easy captives, even though they knew that eternal life and loved ones waited on the other shore.

* * * * * * * *

Lymphoma cancer shortened the life of Bonnie and kept her from reaching the ripe old age that her younger two sisters attained. Had the bad old "C" word not intervened, she probably would have had their same gift of years as well.

Still, she outlasted the doctors' predictions again and again. With a resolute spirit and a zeal to hold onto life, Bonnie learned to live with the cancer lifestyle of chemo and needles and the fatigue that accompanied them.

After chemo subsided, her russet locks grew back in almost snow white. While in one remission she lost her caregiver, Uncle Bill, to a heart attack, but through grief still kept her determination to kick cancer in the butt.

On her final hospital trip she told her nursing-home companions that she'd "be back"—a statement she thoroughly believed. When at age 78 she found herself suddenly transported to the Pearly Gates, Aunt Bonnie probably was the most surprised person in the world. She had no doubt about her eternal destiny; only the timing would have stunned her.

Our family's younger ones, who so luxuriated in the attentions of long-living aunts Mable and Frances, can't imagine what they missed by not knowing the gentle, indulgent Bonnie, the very soul of goodness and quiet wisdom—a person with more capacity for love than just about anyone I ever knew—a veritable embodiment of all the fruit of the Spirit. This was the aunt who baked my favorite chocolate cake every time I visited and selflessly sewed my entire back-to-school wardrobe whenever I spent my week with her each summer.

Matthew, one of the lucky young ones who had conscious memory of Bonnie, called the year of her passing "the worst year of my life". He was 8 at the time, but he summed things up for all us all.

My summer garden in 2009, though drear, managed a commendable crop of beets. For my first time ever, I put up my own "Aunt Bonnie's Beet Pickles" and rejoiced that I at last walked in her mightily capacious footsteps.

* * * * * * * *

After gamely nursing my dad through his Alzheimer's and the diabetic coma that took him down in 1993, Mable revived into a period of triumphant widowhood.

Her secret to conquering grief was to become a "human doing."

That "doing" found her making masterpiece quilts, cross-stitching, presiding over her Sunday-school class, encouraging shut-ins, researching genealogy, "grandmothering" with abandon, and jetting to our home on the East Coast.

She was blessed with fine health and limitless drive, not to mention friends by the bucketloads. On her 90th-birthday celebration in 2001, appropriately 90 people turned out for her party.

But Louis and I knew that we sat on a ticking time-bomb where Mable and Frances, four years older than my mother, were concerned. With both of them in their 90s, and with Aunt Frances not having direct heirs, we knew that our East Coast location soon would be shot through with complications. As Katie left for Baylor and we were empty-nested, we relocated to Texas to watch over our nonagenarian kin.

Only two months after we resettled on "magic" 11th Street in a home diagonal from my mother, her routine yearly physical turned up a heart murmur. Her cardiologist diagnosed her with aortic stenosis and gave her two years at the most.

We had not gotten home before dark, but we had gotten home—in the nick of time.

Mable acted as though her hearing aid was out when the doctor spoke of her short life expectancy. This phenom let nothing stop her—even being put on hospice. The very next Sunday morning—despite pouring rain—she was in her place at church and wholly ready to preside over her class. She was the only member present; the rest had feared the inclement weather.

"Old age must burn and rave at close of day"[2]—another line from the earlier-mentioned poem by Dylan Thomas—surely was written with her in mind. Arm-wrestling a cougar would have been simpler than getting Mable to even give a nod to her heart condition.

She "graduated" (was too well to continue to certify) from

hospice twice and from home-health care twice as well. She fell out of a chair, out of a bed, and heaven knows how many other times she never divulged. Still maintaining her own home, she refused household help, was humiliated when we shared with her part of our supper, and implored us <u>not</u> to open car doors for her. "The Talk" about surrendering her car keys was textbook awful.

But two bad falls in one day's time in January 2005 rapidly sent Mable beyond the pale. She was carried to assisted living and never returned to her "dream home" at 412 South 11th where she and my daddy had handpicked every fireplace stone and overseen every decorative swirl being etched in the ceiling.

When Mable saw she could not recover and continue on as a human doing, she dug in her heels and did a total about-face. She asked to be put to bed, stopped eating, balked at medicines, refused water, and told everyone goodbye. She expected that the end would arrive immediately and that she would instantly be translated to glory to be with God and my daddy.

No such luck.

Rousing from one period of nonresponsiveness, she asked, perturbed and clear as a bell, "Why am I not dead yet?" Ever in control, she seemed dumfounded that Somebody Else got to call the shots in this matter.

Three times Louis and I were summoned and told she was passing. Three times her body rallied. At some points Louis and I believed the undertaker would have to ready three caskets. Almost taken out from the roller-coaster ride of emotions, we were sure we both would perish alongside her.

With both of us at home in a reprieve of sleep and an overnight caregiver standing by, my mother at last got her wish. At 3:45 on the morning of April 7, 2005, the angels made their way into room A112 of Abba Care Assisted Living.

They likely whispered to this stalwart Christian warrior something akin to, "Mable Wheeler, mighty woman of valor, come to Jesus." She gave herself over to their charge.

At 93 1/2 Mable, the last-born of the Miller girls, joined Bonnie, their parents, Bill, Herbert, Grandma and Grandpa Harris, Joe, and of course, my daddy, on heaven's shore.

We expected that Aunt Frances, four years her senior, now would slog through life and be gone within a year.

We underestimated the Miller girls' scrappy middle sister, who for her whole life believed she never had a role. She definitely had one now; she filled it to the uttermost.

* * * * * * *

Make no mistake. Frances, "Middle Red", missed her sister, Mable, immensely.

The two had a curious love-hate relationship. When one bought a brown car, the other bought a brown car. When one made a pink floral quilt, the other made a pink floral quilt. When one crocheted a bedspread, the other did, also, even if working it took seven years. On the other hand, if Mable voted Republican, Frances voted Democrat. Since Mable was a veteran member of First Baptist, Garland, Frances would never consider that church and instead joined Garland's Calvary Baptist across town. Though they might profoundly deny it, each watched over the other's shoulder from stem to stern and never took any action that was not exactly the same or exactly the opposite of the other.

We believed Frances would be lost without Mable—her touch-point, her plumb-line—the one to whom she either copied or bowed her neck against.

But when Mable's passing established her as the matriarch—the grand treasure of our remaining family, Frances did the same thing she did when Herbert was wrenched from her back in 1973 and everyone thought she would perish in grief. She decidedly rose to the occasion.

Still doing water aerobics when she was well into her 90s and still stitching afghans for charity at 99, Frances basked in the attention and care lavished on her as the lone remnant of her generation. She adored realizing that she alone was left to bless the new babies and attend the next generation of weddings and be the repository of the family lore.

When Katie and Casey wed, she served as honorary grandparent—utterly agog that no one but she—the childless sister—could fill that role.

About the same time Mable was diagnosed with aortic stenosis, Frances was diagnosed with atrial fibrillation. Daily she took a formidable total of 21 pills that addressed every ailment from high blood pressure to thyroid condition. That particular potion kept Frances in mint shape for many years.

Just like Mable, Frances fell more times than she had hairs on her head. Most falls, remarkably, had no impact on her. We began to call her the "Teflon Woman" because she was so enduring. Once at Dallas's NorthPark mall she slipped on a step and fell flat on her face. Other than turning technicolor, she had nary a scratch. Again like Mable, she at one point broke a rib but mended quickly as well.

Finally one fall zapped her. At the beauty salon in her assisted-living facility, Frances eased out of the stylist's chair onto the floor and broke her hip. At 99 1/2 that catapulted her into being the oldest person ever to undergo hip-replacement surgery at Baylor Garland Hospital. Her surgeon was ecstatic to have this feather in his cap!

From this incident she would spend the remainder of her years wheelchair-bound, but Frances accepted her situation with patient compliance. Unlike Mable, who caved in when she no longer could function like the indefatigable Energizer bunny, Frances liked nothing better than to be catered to, fawned over, and pampered. At Abba Care, the same compassionate facility that once cared for Mable, Frances reigned from her wheelchair-throne. Utter strangers stopped by her room simply to say they had gazed on a 102-year-old—especially one who was so "with it"—vivacious, cheery, and throbbing with spunk.

At her 102nd birthday party almost every family member popped in to wish her well and have their photo made with her. Bill and Jana's Shelley and her husband, Jarrett, were there with their little Landry, whom Aunt Frances fussed over and wanted to hold. She thrilled over the recent birth of Mia, baby daughter of Mark and Eleene's Marleene and her husband, Josh. Mia and Landry represented the seventh generation down from Grandma Harris.

Mia's arrival was imbued with special significance. Mia was born with a full head of red hair—the first Red-Haired Miller girl in 98 years! About time that gene finally trickled down!

* * * * * * * *

Again, as with Mable, a rip-snorting fall proved to be Aunt Frances' final undoing.

In the wee hours, five weeks after her birthday, Aunt Frances slid out of bed, gashed her leg to the bone, and required 44 stitches. The ensuing, nightmarish emergency room trip depleted her last reserves. On hospice once back at Abba Care, Aunt Frances drifted out of responsiveness and remained that way for a week. As with Mable, she had episodes which prompted the family to be rushed in for goodbyes, only to see her perk up later. No one was shocked to see this gritty steel magnolia "rage, rage against the dying of the light."[3]

The Friday afternoon before Memorial Day, the hospice nurse advised Louis that Frances was taking final breaths. He raced home to get me. We grabbed a quick bite, fed the dog early, shut the house down, and prepared for a long vigil of waiting, just as we'd done repeatedly.

As we entered the room, the nurse advised us, "She's going, but it may be this way for hours."

I sat on her right side and took her hand. My cousin Yvonne was at her left, with Yvonne's husband, Wheat, bolstering her. Louis stood at Frances' feet. We again whispered our love and goodbyes. For a week now Aunt Frances had never responded verbally to anything that had been said to her, but we never doubted she was fully aware of those nearby. Now, in these final moments the two persons who were her next of kin on this earth and our spouses were her lone Send-off Committee—just as it should have been.

Louis, her buddy for these last years of caregiving, had driven her to many a doctor's appointment and had been her right arm in regulating her pills, buying her groceries, and managing her business matters.

We barely had attended her deathwatch for five minutes when Louis spoke up clearly, "Frances, we love you. We'll do our best to carry on."

His was the last voice she heard on this earth. At his sentence trailed off, her breathing stopped. We watched for a subsequent breath. We saw none.

The *chariots and horsemen of Israel* (2 Kings 2:12) had departed with Aunt Frances' spirit. The glad reunion on the other side had begun. We listened carefully to see if perhaps even we could hear the joybells ringing. The last little Miller

Girl was safely home.

A couple of hours later, after the undertaker had left (with one gurney and not three), Louis remarked, "Can't you just imagine what happened when Frances and Herbert saw each other up there? I bet they haven't stopped hugging yet."

Thinking of the two eternal sweethearts—young again, their bodies whole, their minds renewed—reunited after 36 long years apart made me smile through my tears.

In my imagination Uncle Herbert waited at the Gate to lovingly extend his hand and escort Aunt Frances through heaven's portals. As he did so, his voice likely boomed, "Baby, where you been for so long?"

* * * * * * * *

When my mother was in the process of willing herself out of life, she was deliberate in her goodbyes. I listened as she purposefully crafted her final words as each loved one filed in.

One speech particularly struck me. To Matthew, who couldn't be present but who repeatedly called her from his and Marcie's home in Phoenix, she instructed, "Now, Matthew, I want you to be good. You have that little great-granddaughter of mine to think about."

Great-granddaughter? Matthew and Marcie had no children and none on the way. As I heard her directions, I smiled yet wondered whether she perhaps knew something we didn't. After all, in those valedictory moments she was a lot closer to God's omnipotence than any of the rest of us.

Before many weeks passed after Grandma's death, Matthew dialed us up with a giant jolt of news. Marcie was expecting our first grandchild. In the fullness of time their ultrasound showed she *indeed* was carrying a girl.

Matthew remarked that Grandma must have put in her request to God immediately after she got Home.

Caroline Grace Moore, Mable's great-granddaughter, was born January 14, 2006. A highchair sat at our family table to fill the spot left empty by Grandma Wheeler's passing. Caroline was swaddled in a pink afghan Grandma crocheted a couple of years before to leave behind for Matthew's child.

The Lord giveth and the Lord taketh away. Blessed be the name of the Lord!

* * * * * * * *

On one of the episodes when Aunt Frances seemed to be dying and then rallied, Matthew was able to catch a plane flight home.

His tears splashed onto her pillow as he held her flaccid wrist and thanked her for all she'd meant. From Caroline, now 3 1/2, Matthew brought a coloring-book picture that Caroline had made just for Aunt Frances. Though he got no response, Matthew painstakingly described to Aunt Frances every detail of the colored page. A few days later Matthew made a second 24-hour trip home to be a pallbearer.

Aunt Frances had relished her role as surrogate great-grandmother to Caroline. Photos of Matthew's little girl papered a corner of her room. Her pride over outliving Mable and thus getting to be a household name with Caroline was hardly thinly veiled. We were sure she could scarcely wait to get to heaven to boast to Mable with the full report detailing all of Caroline's attributes.

A week to the day after Aunt Frances' funeral, Matthew phoned us one night at bedtime. He had some news. Marcie was expecting again.

The place at our family table vacated by Aunt Frances would be filled with another Moore grandchild.

Just as it had with Mable.

The Lord taketh away; the Lord giveth. Blessed be the name of the Lord! Ryan Jacob Moore was born January 18, 2010.

* * * * * * * *

When they become old enough to understand, I will go on a visit back to Delta County and take Caroline and her little brother, Ryan, and any other grandchildren God may grant us. I will drive down the country lanes of my mother's childhood and ask the youngsters to use their imaginations as they look at the weed-covered fields. I will show them the cherished spots, now bare, in Brushy Mound where the Three Red-Haired Miller Girls grew and thrived. I will ask them to train their ears to listen for the imaginary sounds of little girls at play. I will prod them to climb out of the car and inhale the ineffable sweetness of the country air so far beyond the comprehension of most city children. I will guide them past the vacant lot that once housed the hospital in which Aunt Frances and Grandma Wheeler had their tonsils out without benefit of anesthesia. I will motor by the site of the "River Jordan"—my childhood name for the gin pool where all three Miller Girls were baptized. We will gaze on the place where Granddaddy Miller's lush gardens once fed his family and made his girls believe they were royalty because they had so much good food.

Just as I had once, my grandkiddos probably will listen politely but stare blankly at the empty landscape. Momentarily they may fidget and wonder how soon we can get back home to watch "Dora the Explorer" or "Bob the Builder." It will all seem like so much hoo-haw and fly past them, just as it did me once upon a time.

But then at Christmas or at a family get-together or at just some average dinnertime, we will serve Aunt Bonnie's Beet Pickles or Aunt Frances' Strawberry Cake or the Tomato Preserves like Grandma Harris made.

This will reinforce in their minds that the recipe is tied to a person—a person, though gone, who has more influence on the kind of people they are than they can possibly imagine. *By faith he still speaks, even though he is dead* (Heb. 11:4).

Some day Louis and I and other kin of our generation will be added to *such a great cloud of witnesses* (Heb. 12:1) waiting on the other side. Added to the list of venerated foods may be other country-to-the-bone recipes—Louis' Pumpkin Butter that he made when his garden produced more than ample pumpkins and Kay's Peach Cobbler made for George and Lynda when they visited to discuss the "secret" wedding.

New faces at the table will grow up hearing about the Blackberry Cobbler that Bill and Jana brought to the meal served before Aunt Frances' funeral and Eleene's Old-Fashioned Custard, the first recipe that her future mother-in-law, Yvonne, ever shared with her after she and Mark married.

Though we won't be around to tell the engrossing stories, family lore will preserve them. The recipes from the garden will live on.

A line of poetry from John Donne that Louis and I have a tradition of quoting to each other when one of us is about to travel says, "They who one another keep alive, ne'er parted be."[4]

Because of the recipes that one day will keep our memories vividly alive in the minds of generations yet unborn, we'll never be far away.

[1] Dylan Thomas, "Do Not Go Gentle into That Good Night", quoted in *Americans' Favorite Poems,* Robert Pinsky and Maggie Dietz, eds., (New York: Norton & Company, 2000), 273.
[2] Ibid.
[3] Ibid., 274.
[4] John Donne, "Song", quoted in *The Child from the Sea*, Elizabeth Goudge (New York: Coward-McCann Inc., 1970), 304.

Blackberry Cobbler

2 quarts blackberries
2 cups sugar
1/2 cup all-purpose flour
1 stick butter
1 purchased pie crust, or crust made from your favorite recipe

Spray with cooking oil a 13-by-9-inch baking dish. Spread the blackberries into the dish. Mix sugar and flour, then sprinkle mixture over berries. Slice the stick of butter into 1/2-inch slices, then dot the butter pats over berries, sugar, and flour. Place pie crust strips in a crisscross pattern over the berries. Brush the crust with melted butter; sprinkle with sugar. Bake at 350 degrees until the cobbler is golden brown.

Family Tree
and
Family Album

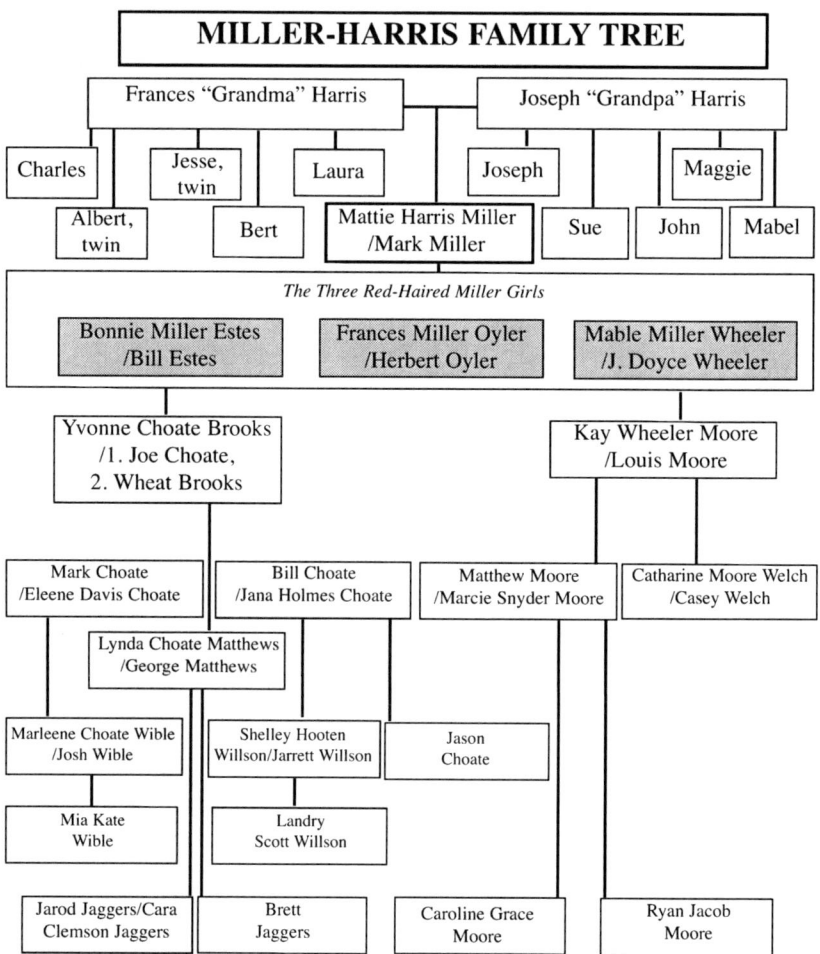

Family Album

Cooper train station, from which Doyce and his dad departed for Austin to get rabies shots for Doyce's dog bite. The building now houses the area's museum.

Delta County Courthouse, at which Frances worked in the county extension office

Grandpa and Grandma Harris in their flower garden with Margaret Miller, a cousin of the Miller Girls

Grandma Harris, right, in four-generation photo with (from left) Bonnie, Yvonne, and Mattie

The Three Red-Haired Miller Girls: from left, Mable, Frances, and Bonnie

Frances in front of Cooper's First National Bank, at which she worked as a teller

Doyce, about the time of the dog bite, poses with his grandfather, James Washington Wheeler.

The inimitable Judy

Frances' Judy is front and center of this joint family Christmas gathering in the 1940s. With Frances and Judy on row 1 is Yvonne. Back row, from left, Doyce, Mable, Herbert, Bonnie, Mattie, Zella, and J.D.

Kay with Mable and Doyce at about the time the birthday cake went unbaked

Kay with Mammaw and Bandad, on the front porch of the little gray house. Katie's wedding reception was held on the site where the gray house once stood.

Frances having breakfast in her kitchen—probably dining on some of her homemade jam

Frances in her wonderful kitchen of knotty pine

Frances and Herbert's bungalow at 202 South Montreal in Oak Cliff, Dallas

Herbert's driftwood collection exhibited in the State Fair of Texas

Herbert, left, and his employees at the Davis Street Drive-In in Oak Cliff

The historic Oak Cliff tornado
(Source: www.1957dallastornado.net)

A successful fishing outing for Herbert

Atop storm cellar at Bonnie and Bill's farm. Kay with cousins Mark, left, and Bill

Louis, below right, and his siblings Robert and Mary with Aunt Tennie at the acreage she and Uncle W.C. had

Louis about the time of his many summer visits to Aunt Tennie and Uncle W.C.'s

Kay, wearing the wedding dress that later disappeared, and her parents at her marriage to Louis in 1969

Kay in floppy brimmed hat she wore to the Kentucky Derby

Herbert's Mesquite Bar-B-Q at the time it opened

Dust Commander storms under the wire in the 1970 Kentucky Derby shocker at which Kay had a historic reporting assignment.

Mable visits in Kay and Louis' townhome about the time of the wedding dress incident.

Gentleman farmer: Louis, with the help of Katie and Matthew, tills the soil for the vegetable garden at the KLMK Farm.

Matthew with Klifford, Victory, and Smurfette in KLMK pasture, below

Katie and Matthew with pumpkins and tomatoes on the steps of the KLMK

Katie and Matthew with their grandmother, Grace Moore, and Pepper the poodle on the front porch of the KLMK

Joe, Yvonne, and Frances visit the KLMK at Thanksgiving.

The Three Red-Haired Miller Girls together at Christmas. From left, Frances, Bonnie, and Mable

Mable in her flower garden at 412 South 11th Street, Garland

Mable at Matthew and Marcie's wedding, 2001

Louis brings in a fresh peach crop from his backyard garden.

Kay picks peaches from an abundant harvest.

Wheat and Yvonne after their 2004 wedding

Katie and Casey with Aunt Frances, who was "honorary grandparent" when the couple wed in 2007

Surveying the cabbage crop

Aunt Frances loved being the doting, substitute great-grandma with Caroline, pictured in her daddy's lap.

Surrounded by four of her great-great-nieces and -nephews is Aunt Frances on her 102nd birthday. From left are Brett, Jarod, Jason, and Shelley.

Aunt Frances meets Shelley and Jarrett's Landry, her great-great-great nephew. Landry is in the 7th generation down from Grandma Harris.

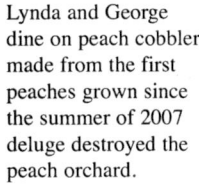

Lynda and George dine on peach cobbler made from the first peaches grown since the summer of 2007 deluge destroyed the peach orchard.

Yvonne meets Marleene and Josh's Mia as grandma Eleene looks on. Flame-haired Mia is Yvonne's great-grand and like Landry is in the 7th generation down from Grandma Harris.

Louis loads up on produce at the Chickasaw farmers' market.

A radiant Lynda and George at their summer 2009 wedding

"Couple" photos: from top, counter-clockwise:
Marleene and Josh Wible, Shelley and Jarrett Willson,
Jarod and Cara Jaggers. At right (top) Matthew and
Marcie Moore, Katie and Casey Welch

Kay and Louis with Caroline

Mark and Eleene with Mia

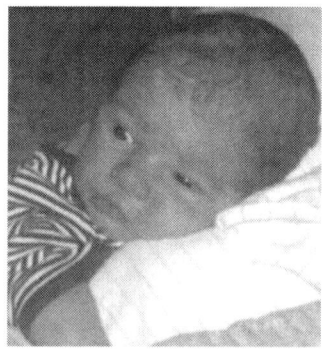

Bill and Jana with Landry

Most recently seated at the
family table:
Ryan Jacob Moore

Recipes

Line drawings of the KLMK Farm, Round Top, TX, and Aunt Bonnie and Uncle Bill's farm, Delta County, TX. Bonnie and Bill are in inset at top right.

Remember the days of old; consider the generations long past. Ask your father and he will tell you, your elders, and they will explain to you (Deut. 32:7).

My mother—Mable Evelyn Miller Wheeler, "Little Red", who took time to *explain* to me, as the above verse mentions

Breakfast Foods

I kick off this recipe section with a collection of breakfast foods from the garden. People often think only of veggie sides when they think of things homegrown, but garden yield has limitless uses. For example friends and family are blessed to be on Bill and Jana's radar screen when their garden has its annual abundance. Often Jana will load someone up with her Zucchini Muffins from their wonderful homegrown zucchini.

Zucchini Muffins

- 2 1/2 cups all-purpose flour
- 2 eggs
- 1 1/4 cups sugar
- 3/4 cup plus 1 tablespoon oil
- 2 1/2 cups grated zucchini
- 2 teaspoons vanilla
- 1 teaspoon salt
- 1 teaspoon baking soda
- 1 teaspoon baking powder
- 1 teaspoon cinnamon
- 1/4 teaspoon nutmeg
- 1 cup buttermilk

In a large bowl combine all ingredients. Mix well. Grease muffin tins. Pour mixture into muffin cups until the cups are 2/3 full. Bake 350 degrees for 25 minutes.

These Potato Pancakes are included in the breakfast section of this cookbook, but they'd be great at any meal and with just about any food item.

Potato Pancakes

6 medium-sized potatoes
1 small onion
2 eggs, slightly beaten
3 tablespoons all-purpose flour
1/4 teaspoon pepper
1 teaspoon salt
1/2 teaspoon baking powder

Peel and grate potatoes and onion. Mix together. Let stand 10 minutes. Drain any liquid that emerges from the mixture. Stir in eggs. Add flour, pepper, salt, and baking powder. Heat small amount of oil in skillet on medium heat. Drop by tablespoonfuls into skillet. Brown on both sides for about 3-4 minutes per side. Drain on paper towel. Serve hot with applesauce, sugar, or cream. Makes 8-10 servings.

Aunt Frances obtained this recipe from the granddaughter of one of her cousins on the Harris side—the great-granddaughter of Mattie's brother Jess Harris. I used the zucchini from my "Chickasaw vegetables" (purchased at a Chickasaw farmers' market) to make Zucchini Bread mini-loaves (baked in mini-loaf pans). They made wonderful hostess gifts and thank-you gifts and sliced up into the perfect size for snacks while we were traveling.

Zucchini Bread

3 eggs, beaten
1 cup oil
1 2/3 cup sugar
1/3 cup brown sugar
2 cups grated zucchini (best to grate in blender)
2 teaspoons vanilla
3 cups all-purpose flour
1 teaspoon baking soda
3 teaspoons cinnamon
1/2 teaspoon baking powder
1 teaspoons salt
1/2 cup chopped pecans

Cut peeled zucchini into 1 1/2-inch cubes; place in blender bowl, add water until zucchini floats freely. Turn on blender for a few seconds until zucchini is grated. Drain through strainer. In large mixing bowl combine beaten eggs, oil, sugar, brown sugar, grated zucchini, and vanilla. In separate bowl combine flour, baking soda, cinnamon, baking powder, and salt. Add to liquid ingredients. Mix well. Add pecans. Grease loaf pans. Fill 2/3 to 3/4 full. Bake at 325 degrees for 1 hour. Remove from pans after cooling 5-10 minutes.

Here is another terrific recipe that we made from our peach crop. Biting into a peach morsel in the midst of these sweet muffins is pure delight.

Fresh Peach Muffins

1 egg
1 cup milk
1/4 cup melted shortening
2/3 cup sugar

1/2 teaspoon salt
1/4 teaspoon cinnamon
1 teaspoon lemon juice
1/4 teaspoon vanilla
2 cups all-purpose flour
3 teaspoons baking powder
1 cup peeled, chopped, fresh peaches

Beat egg. Stir in milk, shortening, sugar, salt, cinnamon, lemon juice, and vanilla. Sift together flour and baking power. Stir into milk mixture until all is blended. Do not overmix. Fold in peaches. Fill greased muffin cups 2/3 full. Bake at 450 degrees for 20 minutes or until brown. Serve warm.

Each one of these mini pecan pies is a taste of Texas. Our paper-shell pecans made a good crop last fall after a two-year absence. You can bet these muffins were among the first recipes we tried with our newly shelled nuts.

Texas Pecan Pie Muffins

1 cup brown sugar
2 eggs
2/3 cup margarine, melted
1 1/2 cups chopped pecans
1/2 cup all-purpose flour

Mix the first three ingredients. Then mix the last two ingredients. Combine the two mixtures. Spoon into muffin cups. Bake at 350 degrees for 25 minutes. Makes 12 muffins.

Caramel Apple Coffee Cake is a favorite for a fall breakfast or Christmas morning breakfast. You can be sure it tastes like caramel apples like you would buy on a stick at the fair.

Caramel Apple Coffee Cake

3 eggs
2 cups sugar
1 1/2 cups oil
2 teaspoons vanilla
3 cups all-purpose flour
1 teaspoon salt
1 teaspoon baking soda
3 cups chopped, peeled apples
1 cup coarsely chopped pecans

Topping:
1/2 cup butter
1/4 cup milk
1 cup packed brown sugar

Beat eggs until foamy; gradually add sugar. Blend in oil and vanilla. Combine flour, salt, and soda; add to egg mixture. Stir in apples and nuts. Pour into greased, 10-inch tube pan; bake at 350 degrees for 1 hour and 15 minutes or until cake tests done. Cool in pan on wire rack for 10 minutes. Remove to serving plate. Topping: Combine all ingredients in a saucepan; boil 3 minutes. Stir constantly. Slowly pour over warm cake (some will run down onto plate). Serves 12-16.

When Caroline has a sleepover with us at our grandparent house in Arizona, I make these Bursting Blueberry Pancakes for her. She often helps by stirring in the cooled milk and eggs, measuring the flour and sugar, or whisking the dry ingredients.

Bursting Blueberry Pancakes

1 cup milk
4 tablespoons (1/2 stick) butter
2 large eggs
1 1/4 cups all-purpose flour
1 tablespoon plus 2 teaspoons sugar
4 teaspoons baking powder
pinch of salt
2 1/2 cups fresh or frozen blueberries
flavorless vegetable oil spray

In small saucepan heat the milk and butter over low heat until the butter melts. Stir to combine, then set aside to cool to room temperature. In a large bowl lightly beat the eggs with a fork. Add the cooled milk mixture and beat well. In another mixing bowl combine flour, sugar, baking powder, and salt; whisk to mix well. Gradually add to the milk and eggs and stir with a spoon just until the batter is combined. Do not overmix. Stir in blueberries. Lightly spray a griddle or large skillet; heat over medium-high heat. When hot ladle batter on in about 1/4-cup amounts. Leave room for spreading. Cook for about 1 minute, or until bubbles on each pancake break and remain open. Turn and cook for 15 or 30 seconds longer or until lightly browned. Serve with syrup. Makes 24 pancakes.

This is wonderful made in individual baking dishes and served for Christmas-morning breakfast.

Baked Apple Pancakes with Caramel Sauce

8 large eggs (or 2 cups egg substitute)
1 cup all-purpose flour

3 tablespoons sugar
1/2 teaspoon salt
1/2 teaspoon ground cinnamon
1 1/2 cups buttermilk
1 teaspoon vanilla
cooking spray
1/2 cup butter
3 apples (Granny Smith or another type of cooking apple), peeled and thinly sliced
1/2 cup brown sugar
1/2 cup chopped pecans
powdered sugar
vanilla ice cream or whipped topping
caramel sauce (purchased—can use caramel topping for ice cream or the type of caramel sauce that one finds near the apples in a grocery produce section)
chopped, toasted pecans

Whisk together eggs and next four ingredients. (Mixture will be lumpy.) Add buttermilk and vanilla. Whisk until batter is blended. Coat 8 (7-by-4-by-1 1/2-inch) oval baking dishes with cooking spray. Divide the butter into 1 tablespoon butter pats. Place 1 butter pat into each dish. Bake at 425 degrees for 3-4 minutes until butter melts. Divide apple slices evenly among the baking dishes. Bake 5 more minutes. Spoon about 1/2 cup batter into each dish. Sprinkle evenly with brown sugar and 1/2 cup chopped pecans. Bake 20 more minutes. Sprinkle pancakes with powdered sugar. Top with a scoop of vanilla ice cream or whipped topping. Drizzle with caramel sauce. Sprinkle with chopped, toasted pecans.

My mother's friend and neighbor, Lillialma Bradfield, was a mentor to her in cooking as well as in many other respects. This slightly older woman took my mother under her wing when Mable moved to Garland as a new bride to J.D. The home the Bradfields owned on Avenue D fronted onto "magic" 11th Street and thus was just across the way from my parents' house at 412 South 11th. In later years, after Mrs. Bradfield and her husband, Bill, passed away, Louis and I were fortunate to own this home for a time and to restore it as part of our desire to regentrify 11th Street in Historic Downtown Garland. Among my mother's recipe collection I was thrilled to find Mrs. Bradfield's recipe for Chocolate Pecan Waffles, which utilizes the fruit of some of those great pecan trees that line our street.

Chocolate Pecan Waffles

1 cup butter, melted
2 squares semi-sweet chocolate
1/2 cup milk
2 eggs, beaten
1 cup sugar
1 3/4 cups flour
1 teaspoon baking powder
1/2 cup chopped pecans

In medium pan melt butter and chocolate squares. Remove from burner and cool. Add milk and beaten eggs. Add sugar, flour, baking powder. Fold in pecans. Pour mixture onto prepared, hot waffle griddle.

Relishes, Appetizers, Jellies

Yvonne furnished this recipe for Tomato Relish; it uses green tomatoes and is totally wonderful.

Tomato Relish

2 gallons (32 cups) green tomatoes, chopped
2 quarts onions, chopped
1 quart bell peppers, chopped
10 hot peppers, chopped
2 tablespoons salt
2 quarts vinegar
6 cups sugar

Into a large kettle place the chopped tomatoes, onions, bell peppers, and hot peppers. In a small bowl mix salt, sugar, and vinegar. Pour over other ingredients. Bring mixture to a boil. Observe when the color of the vegetables changes. At that point reduce heat and simmer for about 5 minutes. Seal in pint jars.

Every year I make bread-and-butter pickles from this recipe. It's a wonderful way for us to use our garden cucumbers, onions, and peppers. With the addition of the red bell pepper these look colorful in the jars. These pickles are absolutely terrific on hamburgers. Everyone raves about them.

Refrigerator Bread-and-Butter Pickles

8 medium cucumbers
6 small yellow onions
1 green bell pepper
1 red bell pepper
1/3 cup salt
2 trays ice cubes
2 1/2 cups sugar
2 1/2 cups apple cider vinegar
1 teaspoon turmeric
1/4 teaspoon whole cloves
1 teaspoon celery seed
1 tablespoon mustard seed

Wash cucumbers. Slice them and the onions. Cut peppers into strips. Place all vegetables into a pot; add salt and ice cubes; cover the pot and let it set three hours. Rinse and drain. In a medium sauce pan bring remaining ingredients to a boil over medium-high heat. Stir occasionally. Once the mixture reaches a boil, remove pan from heat and pour liquid over vegetables. Allow mixture to cool, then pack in clean, heat-proof jars and refrigerate.

Aunt Bonnie's Beet Pickles premiered in my first cookbook, *Way Back in the Country*. They graced every holiday table while I was growing up. Often Aunt Bonnie sent home with us jars of these wonderfully sweet, tangy pickles. Earlier in this book I mentioned my great pride at being able to make these with beets from my own garden. I was thrilled to be able to serve Beet Pickles at our 2009 family Christmas lunch.

Bonnie's Beet Pickles

1 gallon beets, quartered
2 cups sugar
1 stick cinnamon
3 1/2 cups vinegar
1 tablespoon allspice
1 1/2 cups water

In a large saucepan in boiling water cook beets until tender. In a small saucepan mix the sugar, cinnamon, vinegar, allspice, and 1 1/2 cups water. Simmer this mixture for 15 minutes. Add beets and boil 5 minutes. Fill jars and seal. Makes about 4 pint jars.

Marleene furnished this Salsa recipe that she says originated with Josh's Aunt Melissa.

Salsa

4-5 whole tomatoes (or 1 28-ounce can diced or whole tomatoes, drained)
1/2 onion, chopped
handful of chopped cilantro
2 tablespoons apple cider vinegar
1-3 tablespoons chopped jalapeños
1 teaspoon sugar
1 tablespoon salt
1/2 teaspoon cumin
1/2 teaspoon garlic powder
juice of two lemons

Put all ingredients into a blender and blend until smooth.

For several years now Marleene has been bringing this Bread Bowl as an appetizer to our family Christmas event. Family members stand around and graze over this until lunch is served. It originated with her sister-in-law, Dawn Wible.

Dawn's Bread Bowl

1 (16-ounce) sweet round bread loaf (tested with King's Hawaiian)
1 (12-pack) sweet bread rolls (tested with King's Hawaiian)
2 (8-ounce) packages cream cheese, softened
1 (8-ounce) container sour cream
1/2 bundle green onions, chopped
1/2 jar dried beef, chopped
1/2 teaspoon garlic powder
salt and pepper to taste
dash paprika

Cut out center of bread bowl. Retain center pieces that have been cut out. Slice center into 1-inch pieces; also slice rolls into 1-inch pieces. Mix cream cheese and sour cream together; add green onion and dried beef. Sprinkle in garlic powder and salt and pepper. Mix everything together until smooth. Pour dip into bread bowl and sprinkle top with paprika. Bake at 350 degrees for 35 minutes or until hot.

Some friends become like family. My friend, Mary Ann Vessel, and I met in junior-high school and daydreamed of what life would be like when we were married ladies with kids. Later, after all my years away from Garland, I was privileged to reconnect with Mary Ann when Louis and I moved back to the "green, green grass of home". We had granddaughters born in the same year and enjoy swapping yarns about our amazing girls. Here is a recipe from a gift of Sweet Garlic Dills that Mary Ann brought me.

Sweet Garlic Dills

1 gallon dill pickles (concession-stand style), drained and cut into chunks
5 pounds sugar
1 (2-ounce) bottle Tabasco sauce
2 clusters garlic, sliced

Mix together in a large plastic dishpan. Leave on counter for 24 hours covered with a cloth. Stir often. Put in jars and refrigerate.

I made this Fresh Garden Salsa for the fiesta we tossed when Katie graduated in 2009 with her doctorate. All ingredients were straight from our garden—so fresh!

Fresh Garden Salsa

18 ripe tomatoes
3-6 hot peppers, to taste
3 large onions
2 green peppers
1 cup vinegar
2 tablespoons cumin
1 1/2 tablespoons salt
1 small can tomato paste

Chop vegetables and put in food processor to process finely. Return to a large kettle and add all other ingredients. Cook until all vegetables are tender. Mixture may be placed into sterile jars and processed for 15 minutes in boiling-water bath. May also be packed into airtight containers and frozen. Refrigerate before serving.

I consider peach preserves to be the absolute best thing that can be put up with a good crop of peaches. Here's the best recipe I've found.

Peach Preserves

8 cups peaches, peeled, pitted, and sliced (about 4 pounds)
2 tablespoons fresh lemon juice
1 (3-ounce) package powdered pectin
7 cups sugar
1/4 teaspoon almond extract

Combine peaches, lemon juice, and pectin in a large pot or Dutch oven. Bring to a rolling boil and stir gently. Add sugar and return to rolling boil. Boil hard for 1 minute, stirring constantly. Remove from heat. Skim any foam. Add almond extract and mix. Pour into hot jars; leave 1/4-inch headspace. Adjust caps and process for 10 minutes in boiling-water bath. Makes about 6 12-ounce jars.

This simple way of preserving peaches makes a great Christmas gift.

Honey-Peach Butter

10 pounds peaches, peeled and chopped
1/2 cup water
4 1/2 cups sugar
1 1/2 cups honey

In large kettle cook the peaches in water until the peaches are soft. Press through a sieve or food mill. Measure 12 cups pulp; discard liquid; return to kettle. Add sugar and honey. Cook, stirring often, until mixture thickens, about 1 1/4 hours. Stir more frequently as it thickens to prevent sticking. Pour hot mixture into hot jars; leave

1/4-inch headspace. Adjust caps. Process for 10 minutes in a boiling-water bath. Makes 6 pints.

Here's another great flavor combination—pumpkins and apricots. This spread has the consistency of apple butter and a mellow, sweet-tart taste. Spread it on biscuits, muffins, or toast, or serve it as an accompaniment to roasted meats. It also makes a wonderful hostess gift.

Pumpkin-Apricot Butter

>1/2 pound dried apricots
>1 1/2 cups water
>2 cups cooked, mashed pumpkin
>1 (3-inch) cinnamon stick
>grated rind of 1 lemon
>2 1/4 cups sugar

Combine apricots and water in a small bowl; cover and let stand overnight. Drain apricots, reserving water. Cut apricots into thin strips and set aside. Combine reserved water, pumpkins, cinnamon stick, and lemon rind in a large, heavy saucepan; cover and simmer 20 minutes, stirring occasionally. Add reserved apricots and sugar, stirring until well-blended. Bring to a boil; reduce heat, and simmer 30 minutes or until mixture thickens. Remove from heat and discard cinnamon stick. Pour hot pumpkin mixture into hot sterilized jars, leaving 1/4-inch headspace. Cover at once with metal lids and screw on bands. Process in boiling-water bath for 10 minutes. Yields 2 pints.

Louis' abundant grapevines in the back yard sent us scurrying to find an easy grape jelly recipe. We made volumes from one summer's yield. To keep timing prompt use two people when you prepare this recipe on the next page.

Grape Jelly

5 cups prepared juice from fresh grapes
1 (1 3/4-ounce) package powdered fruit pectin
   (tested with SURE.JELL)
7 cups (3 pounds) sugar

Measure sugar and set aside. Mix powdered fruit pectin with juice in pan. Bring quickly to a hard boil stirring occasionally. At once add sugar. Bring to a full rolling boil (a boil that cannot be stirred down). Boil hard for 1 minute. Remove from heat. With metal spoon skim off foam. Pour into prepared jars. Wipe rim with clean damp cloth. Place lid on and screw band on tight but not too tight. Process in water bath or steam canner for 10 minutes. Remove and invert jar and set on newspaper. When sealed stand upright to cool. Yields 8 cups jelly.

For pumpkin butter that makes up quickly, here's a fabulous recipe from the *Houston Chronicle* files.

Microwave Pumpkin Butter

1/4 cup dark brown sugar
2 tablespoons granulated sugar
1/4 cup water
1/2 teaspoon each allspice and cinnamon
1/4 teaspoon each ginger, cloves, and nutmeg
1 1/2 cups cooked, mashed pumpkin

Combine sugars, water, and spices in 4-cup glass measure. Microwave 3 minutes on high. Add pumpkin; microwave 5 minutes on high. Cool and refrigerate. Makes 2 cups.

Salads

Vegetable gardens are simply salads waiting to happen. The possibilities are limitless! Here are a few favorites that are byproducts of our (and others') garden yields—starting with this first "can't-beat" combination. With golden kernels fresh from the cob and vibrant red cherry-tomato halves, Corn and Tomato Salad is as colorful as it is delicious. The sweetness of the corn makes it a kids' favorite, too.

Corn and Tomato Salad

4 ears yellow corn, shucked
1 pint cherry tomatoes, with tomatoes halved
1/2 cup diced Monterey jack cheese
1/4 cup diced red onion
2 tablespoons vegetable oil
2 teaspoons lime juice
1/2 teaspoon cumin
1/2 teaspoon sugar
1/4 teaspoon salt
1 garlic clove, crushed
cilantro sprigs, optional

In large pot of boiling, salted water cook corn 4 minutes; drain. When corn is cool enough to handle, hold corn over bowl and cut kernels from cobs. Add tomatoes, cheese, and onion to bowl. Toss to combine. Combine oil, lime juice, cumin, sugar, salt, and garlic in jar with tight-fitting lid. Shake; pour over vegetables and stir to combine. Sprinkle with cilantro sprigs, if desired. Makes 5 1/4 cups.

We tried this recipe the first summer our garden produced cabbages en masse. Garden Slaw featured below is the best slaw recipe I can ever recall.

Garden Slaw

3 cups shredded cabbage
2 tablespoons chopped carrot
1/2 cup mayonnaise
1/2 cup sour cream
2 teaspoons sugar
1 tablespoon vinegar
1 cup salad oil
1 tablespoon syrup
1/2 teaspoon salt
pepper, celery seed, dry mustard (to taste)

Combine all ingredients and mix well. Cover and refrigerate for about four hours or overnight. Makes 8-10 servings.

When I served this Crisp 'n Crunchy Salad to Aunt Frances, she responded, "This tastes just like one Mama used to make." It makes great use of apples from the garden.

Crisp 'n Crunchy Salad

1 medium golden apple, chopped
1 medium red apple, chopped
2 celery ribs, thinly sliced
1/2 cup walnuts, chopped
1/2 cup golden raisins
1/4 cup honey

In a bowl combine the apples, celery, walnuts, and raisins. Add the honey and mix well. Serve immediately. Serves 6.

Corn Bread Salad capitalizes on fresh tomatoes and whole-kernel corn off the cob.

Corn Bread Salad

1 (8-ounce) box packaged corn bread mix,
    cooked, cooled, and cut into 1/2-inch squares.
1 onion, chopped
3 hard-boiled eggs, chopped
3 tomatoes, chopped
1 1/2 cups chopped celery
1 1/2 cups fresh corn (or 1 15-ounce can whole-
    kernel corn, drained)
2 cups chopped, cooked ham
1 (16-ounce) bottle Catalina salad dressing

Mix all ingredients together. Add Catalina dressing; toss, and serve.

Yvonne furnished this recipe for Copper Carrot Pennies, a dish which I first began appreciating when our friend Lori Haaland prepared it for us during our Houston days. I first dined on it when we joined the Haaland family on their boat on Lake Marble Falls (TX).

Copper Carrot Pennies

4 cups sliced carrots, cooked
1 medium green pepper, sliced
1 medium onion, sliced
1 (10 1/2-ounce) can tomato soup

1/2 cup oil
1 cup sugar
3/4 cup vinegar
1 teaspoon prepared mustard
1 teaspoon Worcestershire sauce
salt and pepper to taste

Layer alternately in a dish the cooked carrots, green pepper, and onion. Combine and blend well the tomato soup, salad oil, sugar, vinegar, prepared mustard, Worcestershire sauce, and salt and pepper. Pour over the vegetables and refrigerate. Serves 10.

Fern Hammock, one of my mother's best friends from church and later a friend of Aunt Frances when both lived at Abba Care, popularized this Overnight Coleslaw. She wrote that before she retired, when her office had a covered-dish get-together, she was always asked to bring her tangy slaw.

Overnight Coleslaw

12 cups (1 medium head) shredded cabbage
1 green pepper, chopped
1 medium red onion, chopped
2 carrots, shredded
1 cup sugar
2 teaspoons sugar
1 teaspoon dry mustard
1 teaspoon celery seed
1 teaspoon salt
1 cup vinegar
3/4 cup oil

In a large bowl combine the first four ingredients. Sprinkle mixture with sugar; set aside. In saucepan, combine last five ingredients.

Bring to a boil. Remove from the heat and pour over vegetables. Stir to cover evenly. Cover and refrigerate overnight. Stir well before serving. Makes 12-16 servings.

This Broccoli and Cranberry Salad is a derivation of Marcie's to-die-for Broccoli Salad introduced in *Way Back in the Country*. The addition of the sweetened dried cranberries makes it colorful—lovely for a Christmas covered-dish meal or any time.

Broccoli and Cranberry Salad

> 5 cups broccoli florets, cut into 1/2-inch pieces
> 1/2 cup chopped red onion
> 1 cup shredded Cheddar cheese
> 1 cup cooked and crumbled bacon pieces
> 1 cup sunflower kernels
> 1 cup sweetened dried cranberries (tested with
>   Ocean Spray Craisins)
> 1 cup nonfat or lowfat salad dressing or mayonnaise
> 1/4 cup sugar
> 2 tablespoons red wine vinegar
> 1/2 teaspoon salt
> 1/4 teaspoon pepper

Combine all salad ingredients (first six ingredients) in a large bowl; mix well. Combine dressing ingredients (last five ingredients) in a small bowl. Mix thoroughly; use a fork or wire whisk. Add dressing to salad and mix well. Refrigerate 1 hour. Makes 8-10 servings.

Speaking of holiday salads, you can deck your holiday dinner table with this winning Italian Vegetable Toss, a vegetable and pasta medley.

Italian Vegetable Toss

1 1/2 cups shell macaroni
2 cups broccoli flowerets
1 cup cauliflower flowerets
1 cup sliced fresh mushrooms
1 (6-ounce) can artichoke hearts, drained, rinsed, and chopped
1 cup sliced pitted ripe black olives
1/2 cup chopped green onion
2/3 cup Italian salad dressing
1 medium avocado, seeded, peeled, and sliced
1 medium tomato, seeded and chopped

Cook macaroni according to package directions; drain. Rinse with cold water; drain well. In a large bowl combine macaroni, broccoli flowerets, cauliflower flowerets, sliced mushrooms, artichoke hearts, black olives, and chopped green onion. Toss with Italian dressing. Cover and chill several hours. At serving time toss vegetable mixture with avocado and tomato. Makes 12-16 servings.

If you really want to take a different kind of salad to a covered-dish event, I suggest you try White Bean Salad with Asparagus. It's healthy, fiber-ific, and colorful.

White Bean Salad with Asparagus

8 stalks green asparagus, tough ends removed
1 (15-ounce) can white beans, rinsed and drained
1 orange bell pepper, seeded and chopped
1/2 red onion, finely chopped
2 tablespoons olive oil
2 tablespoons freshly squeezed lemon juice
1 teaspoon Dijon mustard

salt and pepper to taste
1 cup leafy salad greens (such as romaine lettuce or spinach), loosely packed

Cut asparagus into 1-inch pieces. In vegetable steamer set into large saucepan, lightly steam for 2-3 minutes. Set aside to cool. In large bowl combine white beans, orange pepper, and red onion. Gently toss in asparagus. In separate bowl whisk together olive oil, lemon juice, mustard, salt, and pepper. Gently toss dressing into salad. Adjust seasonings to taste. Line salad bowl with leafy greens. Top greens with white bean salad. Serve with hearty whole-grain bread. Makes 5 servings.

A great way to get your black-eyed peas on New Year's Day besides the traditional veggie side recipe is this Hot Bacon and Black-Eyed Pea Salad.

Hot Bacon and Black-Eyed Pea Salad

1 (10-ounce) package frozen black-eyed peas
   (or 1 1/2 cups dried peas that have been cooked)
1/4 cup sugar
1/4 cup vinegar
1/4 cup water
8 slices bacon
1 small head cauliflower, broken into small flowerets
1/2 cup diced celery
4 green onions with tops, chopped
1 (2-ounce) jar diced pimiento, drained
1 tablespoon brown sugar
2 tablespoons vinegar
1/2 teaspoon salt

Cook peas according to package directions. Omit bacon and salt. Drain well. Combine peas and next three ingredients. Stir well. Cover and chill 3 hours. Add cauliflower, celery, and onions. Cook bacon until crisp; drain well, reserving 2 tablespoons drippings in pan. Crumble bacon and set aside. In small saucepan make dressing of brown sugar, vinegar, and salt. Warm on stove. Gently stir hot dressing into vegetable mixture. Add bacon and serve.

This is the Sunshine Gelatin Salad I mentioned that I served my parents in the traumatic hours after the great wedding dress/dry-cleaners revelation (Chapter 9).

Sunshine Gelatin Salad

1 (3-ounce) box lemon gelatin
1/2 cup shredded carrots (about 2 small carrots)
1 (8-ounce) can crushed pineapple, drained, with
   juice reserved
1/2 cup grated Cheddar cheese
1/4 cup green olives, thinly sliced
1/4 cup shredded cabbage

Drain crushed pineapple; in a 1-cup measuring cup reserve juice. In a medium pan prepare lemon gelatin according to directions on box. After gelatin is dissolved in boiling water, fill with water the measuring cup containing pineapple juice until combined liquid measures one cup. Stir into hot water in which gelatin has been dissolved. Pour liquid mixture into mold. Chill in refrigerator until mixture starts to thicken. Gently fold in carrots, pineapple, cheese, olives, and cabbage. Chill until set. Turn out of mold onto lettuce-lined plate or tray. Serves 8.

In Matthew and Marcie's Phoenix back yard we encountered a new kind of garden—a citrus grove. Buckets of lemons, oranges, and grapefruits could be picked just by stepping a few feet from their door. Amazing! One day when we brought home a piled-high box of oranges, I tried orange segments in this recipe I'd had in my files forever. Tangy Orange and Pecan Salad is a marvelous dish combining many of my favorite things. It would be a stunner at a Christmas buffet.

Tangy Orange and Pecan Salad

 4 navel oranges
 1 lemon
 1 tablespoon sugar
 1 teaspoon cinnamon
 1 teaspoon salt
 1 tablespoon olive oil
 1 cup broken pecans
 1 (16-ounce) bag romaine lettuce, washed, dried, and chopped (about 12 packed cups)
 1/3 cup chopped fresh cilantro leaves
 2 tablespoons grated Parmesan cheese

Peel 3 oranges with a knife; take care to remove the white outer membrane. Separate orange into sections; use knife to trim away remaining membranes. Set orange sections aside; cover with plastic wrap and refrigerate for several hours, if desired. Into a small bowl squeeze juice from remaining orange and from the lemon. Whisk with sugar, cinnamon, salt, and oil. Place pecans in nonstick skillet and toast over low heat a minute or so until nuts are fragrant and slightly crisp. Remove from heat and set aside. Can be prepared several hours ahead. To serve whisk dressing. Place lettuce in large serving bowl; toss with dressing and adjust seasonings if needed. Top with orange segments, pecans, Parmesan, and cilantro. Makes 8 servings.

Lori Haaland also introduced me to Potato-Cucumber Salad Casserole. It's a perfect summer-day dish.

Potato-Cucumber Salad Casserole

4-5 potatoes, sliced, boiled, and cooled
1-2 cucumbers, peeled and sliced thin
1-2 onions (red or green), chopped
1 small container of sour cream
3/4 cup mayonnaise
1/8 teaspoon Worcestershire sauce
1/2 teaspoon celery seed

Layer potatoes, cucumbers, and onions. Stir Worcestershire sauce and celery seed into mayonnaise and sour cream mixture. Spread mayonnaise mixture on top of the vegetable layers. Refrigerate overnight.

When Louis and I first moved to Louisville after our marriage, Tex-Mex restaurants in the city were few, if any. In self-defense I dug and dug until I found this Guacamole recipe to try to satisfy our Texas tastebuds. I've made it hundreds of times, most recently at the fiesta we tossed for Katie when she received her Ph.D.

Guacamole

2 medium ripe avocados, seeded, peeled, and mashed
1 tablespoon minced onion
1 clove garlic, minced
1/4 teaspoon chili powder
1/4 teaspoon salt
1/3 cup mayonnaise
6 sliced cooked bacon, crumbled (can use turkey bacon)

In a small bowl combine avocado, onion, garlic, and seasonings. Spread top with mayonnaise; seal to edges of bowl. Chill. At serving time stir mayonnaise into mixture and stir in bacon. Serves 4.

Once when Louis received a less-than-ideal cholesterol reading at his annual physical exam, we began pushing fish like crazy. This Tuna Grape Salad recipe furnished by the Chickasaw Nation Nutrition Services helped in that regard.

Tuna Grape Salad

2 (4-ounce) cans chunk light tuna, drained
2 cups green or red grapes, halved
1/4 cup plain fat-free yogurt
1/4 cup lite mayonnaise
2 teaspoons yellow curry powder
1/4 cup almond slivers
2 tablespoons onion, minced
1 cup celery, diced

Mix all ingredients. Serve with crackers or toast.

Louis and I love to go on winter picnics. This Crunchy Vegetable Salad accompanied French Onion Soup on one of these adventures.

Crunchy Vegetable Salad

2 cups each cauliflowerets and broccoli florets
2 carrots, thinly sliced
1 small zucchini, sliced
1 small red onion chopped
1 cup fat-free Italian dressing

Combine all ingredients and toss. Refrigerate. Serves 4-6.

Beverages, Soups, Stews

This vibrant, nonalcoholic drink is absolutely incredible with tomatoes fresh-plucked from their vines. The finished product can be seasoned with a squeeze of lemon and a squirt of hot pepper sauce.

Tomato Mary

    10 tomatoes, sliced
    1/4 cup vinegar
    1 teaspoon sugar
    1 teaspoon salt
    1 bay leaf
    2 shoots celery leaves
    2 slices sweet onion

Bring all ingredients to a boil; then reduce heat and simmer for 30 minutes. Strain and seal in sterilized pint jars or refrigerate as long as 5 days. Serve over ice in a tall glass garnished with a celery stick or sprig of herbs.

When I first encountered the idea of hot cucumber soup, I wasn't sure I'd like this flavor. After all, isn't the simile *as cool a cucumber*? But once we sampled the soup produced from the recipe on the next page, we were hooked.

Hot Cucumber Soup

2 teaspoons butter
1 cucumber
2 cups chicken stock
2 green onions
1/2 teaspoon seasoned salt
pinch nutmeg
2 tablespoons plain yogurt
2 teaspoons fresh mint leaves

In large saucepan melt butter. Peel cucumber and cut in half lengthwise. Remove seeds and cut into thin slices. Sauté for 2 minutes. Chop onions; add them with chicken stock and spices to the pan. Simmer 5 minutes. Serve hot topped with yogurt and mint.

Here is another recipe we found to use produce from the Chickasaw farmers' market.

Butternut Squash Soup

2 tablespoons butter
1 onion, chopped
1 butternut squash, peeled
6 cups chicken broth
1 cup milk
1/4 teaspoon nutmeg
1 teaspoon salt
1/4 teaspoon pepper
shredded Cheddar cheese
dash of brown sugar

In a large kettle melt butter. Add onion. Cook 8 minutes or until onion is translucent. Cut squash into chunks. Add squash to the kettle. Add chicken broth. Cook until squash is tender. Remove squash chunks and place in blender to puree. Return blended squash to pot. Stir in milk; season with nutmeg, salt, and pepper. Allow to cook on low heat for about 10 minutes. Serve with a sprinkling of shredded cheese and dash of brown sugar on the top of each serving of soup.

This Chicken Corn Chowder is awesome served with a green salad and a loaf of dark bread. For a vegetarian soup you can omit the bacon and chicken and substitute vegetable broth.

Chicken Corn Chowder

6 slices bacon
1 pound boneless/skinless chicken breast
3/4 cup onion, finely chopped
3/4 cup celery, finely chopped
3 cups chicken broth
4 cups fresh corn (canned or frozen can be subbed)
2 cups diced potatoes
1/2 teaspoon salt, optional
1 cup half and half (can use skim milk)
parsley to taste
1/8 teaspoon white pepper

Cook bacon in large kettle or Dutch oven. Remove bacon and reserve 2 tablespoons grease. In grease cook chicken, onion, and celery for 15-20 minutes or until tender. Stir frequently. In blender combine 1 cup chicken broth and 2 cups corn. Blend until smooth. Pour into pan with chicken and vegetables. Add potatoes, 2 cups chicken broth, and remaining corn. Add salt. Bring to a boil and lower heat to simmer for 20 minutes or until potatoes are tender. Add half and half, parsley, and pepper. Simmer 2-3 minutes. Stir in bacon and serve.

You can almost taste the freshness of a summer garden just from reading the title of this great soup served cold. Grabbing the first green tomatoes off the vine is wonderful because you don't have to wait for them to ripen.

Green Gazpacho Soup

1 green pepper, seeded, chopped
1 medium cucumber, peeled
1 ripe avocado, peeled
3 medium-sized green tomatoes (or the least-ripe tomatoes you can find), cored and chopped
1/2 cup cilantro leaves
1 small onion, peeled, quartered
2 cloves garlic, peeled
6 tablespoons fresh lime juice
2 tablespoons olive oil
2 teaspoons sugar
1 1/2 teaspoons ground cumin
1 1/2 teaspoons salt
1/8 teaspoon cayenne

Mince 1/2 cup green pepper; set aside for garnish. Place remaining pepper in large bowl. Cut cucumber lengthwise in half. With spoon remove and discard seeds. Coarsely chop cucumber. Mince 1/4 cup cucumber; set aside for garnish. Add remaining cucumber to pepper in large bowl. Cut avocado into chunks. In large bowl add avocado, tomatoes, cilantro, onion, garlic, lime juice, olive oil, sugar, cumin, salt, and cayenne to cucumbers and pepper; toss. In batches puree vegetable mixture in food processor until smooth. Transfer to another large bowl or 8-cup measuring cup. Stir in 1 1/2 cups cold water; cover and refrigerate 2 hours to allow flavors to blend and soup to chill. Ladle soup into bowls, garnish with additional cilantro leaves, minced green pepper, and cucumber. Serve chilled.

My other native state—Colorado, from which my birth-family hails—is famed for its excellent potatoes. Here is a potato soup recipe I acquired while I visited in Colorado one time. The soup is absolutely loaded with healthy fresh vegetables. My husband pronounced it the best soup he'd ever eaten.

Rocky Mountain Potato Chowder

1/4 pound (4 to 6 slices) turkey bacon, cut into small pieces
1 bunch green onions, thinly sliced, white parts separated from green tops
3 1/2 cups chicken broth
1 1/2 pounds (3 to 4) potatoes, peeled and diced
1 cup sliced carrots
1 red bell pepper or 1 1/2 pounds tomatoes, seeded and diced
1 medium zucchini, sliced
1 cup corn kernels
1 1/2 teaspoons dried thyme leaves
2 cups shredded cooked turkey or chicken
2 cups lowfat milk plus 2 tablespoons cornstarch
salt and pepper to taste

In heavy pot over medium heat brown bacon. Pour off fat, if any remains. Add white and light green parts of onions (reserve 1/2 cup green tops); cook and stir 1 minute. Add broth and potatoes; cover and cook 15 minutes or until potatoes are almost tender. Add carrots; cook 5 minutes more. Add bell pepper, zucchini, corn, and thyme; cook until vegetables are tender. Add turkey or chicken and reserved onion tops. Mix milk with cornstarch; add to pot. Bring to a boil; stir constantly about 1 minute until soup thickens slightly. Season with salt and pepper. Makes 6 servings.

Lynda acclaimed this soup a hit in her office where she works as an administrator for the Mesquite (TX) school district.

Potato Soup

1 medium diced onion
3 1/2-4 (14-ounce) cans fat-free chicken broth
1 (32-ounce) bag frozen diced hashbrown potatoes
1 package fat-free country gravy mix

Sauté onions while you bring broth to a boil. Reserve about a cup of broth for mixing with gravy mix later. Add onions and potatoes to remaining broth. Mix gravy mix package into cup of reserved hot broth and return to pot of soup (dilutes easier this way). Cook until potatoes are tender. If you desire add 3-4 slices of processed cheese loaf (tested with Velveeta) at the end for a creamier soup. You can also garnish with shredded cheese, chives, and/or bacon bits.

I acquired this Cabbage Sausage Soup recipe from a woman who described it as "perfect for hurried cooks" (doesn't that categorize most of us?). After preparing it while I was in a time squeeze many times, I agree with her assessment.

Cabbage Sausage Soup

4 cups chicken broth
1 small cabbage, chopped (about 10 cups)
1 medium onion, chopped
1/2 pound fully cooked smoked sausage, halved
  lengthwise and sliced
1/2 cup all-purpose flour
1 1/2 teaspoons salt
1/4 teaspoon pepper
1 cup milk

In a large kettle or Dutch oven bring to a boil the broth, cabbage, and onion. Reduce heat; cover, and simmer for 10-15 minutes or until cabbage is tender. Add sausage; heat through. In a bowl combine the flour, salt, and pepper. Gradually add milk and stir until smooth. Gradually stir into soup. Bring to a boil; cook and stir for 2 minutes or until thickened. Makes 8 servings (about 2 quarts).

This Turkey Cabbage Stew falls into the same category. It would score points with my husband for its stovetop cookability. Truly it can be ready in 30 minutes or less.

Turkey Cabbage Stew

1 pound ground turkey
1 medium onion, chopped
3 garlic cloves, minced
4 cups chopped cabbage
2 medium carrots, sliced
1 (28-ounce) can diced tomatoes, undrained
3/4 cup water
1 tablespoon brown sugar
1 tablespoon white vinegar
1 teaspoon salt
1 teaspoon dried oregano
1/4 teaspoon dried thyme
1/4 teaspoon pepper

In large saucepan cook turkey, onion, and garlic over medium heat or until meat no longer is pink; drain. Add remaining ingredients. Bring to a boil; cover and simmer for 6-8 minutes or until the vegetables are tender. Makes 6 servings.

Eleene loves to tell stories about growing up with a family garden nearby. At dinnertime her mother would send her out to the garden to pick for dinner fresh vegetables. She still loves to use fresh vegetables in her cooking, as evidenced by her two recipes below: Cheesy Potato Broccoli Soup and Hearty Country Beef Stew.

Cheesy Potato Broccoli Soup

3 cups peeled, cubed potatoes (about 1 pound of potatoes)
1 cup fresh or frozen chopped broccoli, thawed
1/2 cup chopped carrots
1/2 cup chopped onions
1/2 cup water
1/4 teaspoon salt (or to taste)
1 (14 1/4-ounce) can no-salt-added chicken broth
1 tablespoon black pepper
3 tablespoons flour
1 1/2 cups 1-percent or skim milk
6 to 8 ounces reduced-fat process cheese spread, cubed (tested with Velveeta)
dried crushed red pepper (optional)
dried red chili peppers (optional)

In a large Dutch oven combine first eight ingredients. Bring to boil; cover, reduce heat, and simmer 20 minutes. Combine milk and flour; stir with a whisk until smooth. Add milk mixture and cheese to vegetable mixture in Dutch oven. Cook uncovered over medium heat, stirring constantly, until cheese melts and mixture thickens. If desired, sprinkle with crushed red pepper and garnish with dried chili peppers. Makes about 7 (1-cup) servings.

Hearty Country Beef Stew

2 pounds cubed stew meat
butter or olive oil
1 medium onion, diced
1 green pepper, diced
1 or 2 tablespoons chili powder
1 teaspoon garlic powder
1 (14 1/2-ounce) can green beans, drained (can substitute fresh
   green beans)
3 or 4 carrots, sliced bite size
1 cup frozen or canned whole-kernel corn, drained
4 or 5 medium new potatoes, cut in bite-size chunks, with skin on
1 cup celery, diced
2 (14 1/2-ounce) cans stewed tomatoes, with liquid
1 (46-ounce) can tomato juice
1 teaspoon salt
1 tablespoon black pepper

Brown stew meat on all sides in butter or olive oil in large skillet. Use slotted spoon to remove meat from skillet; allow meat drippings to remain in skillet. Place meat in 6-quart crockpot. Add diced onion and green pepper to skillet and sauté for about 5 minutes. Add entire contents of skillet to crockpot with meat. To crockpot add salt, pepper, chili powder, garlic powder, and all other prepared vegetables. Add tomatoes and tomato juice into crockpot; stir to combine ingredients. (This will fill a 6-quart slow cooker. You may have to reduce amount of potatoes and/or carrots if you use a smaller pot). Cook on low for 6 hours. (Do not remove slow-cooker lid during cooking, or cooking time may have to be increased because of loss of heat). After 6 hours cooking on low, turn crockpot on high setting and cook final 2 hours. Add salt and pepper to taste and serve.

This Easy Vegetable Soup will always be special to me because I prepared it for the first time my birthmother, Eleanor, and her husband, Charles, visited us in Texas. Although that time I prepared it in summer, it also bespeaks of an autumn day.

Easy Vegetable Soup

- 1 pound ground beef or ground turkey
- 1 cup chopped onion
- 1/8 teaspoon garlic powder
- 1 cup sliced carrots
- 1 cup sliced celery
- 1/4 cup uncooked regular rice
- 2 (16-ounce) cans stewed tomatoes
- 3 1/2 cups water
- 5 beef bouillon cubes
- 1 tablespoon parsley flakes
- 1 teaspoon salt
- 1/4 teaspoon basil
- 1/8 teaspoon pepper
- 1 cup frozen mixed vegetables, unthawed
- 1 (10 3/4-ounce) can low-sodium tomato soup

Cook ground beef or turkey; drain fat. Add all ingredients except frozen vegetables and tomato soup. Cook covered for 40 minutes. Add frozen vegetables and tomato soup. Cook additional 10 minutes. Serves 10-12.

Vegetable Sides

What joy I had finding this Okra Creole recipe among Aunt Frances' collection! The recipe card had browned edges—a sign of much use.

Okra Creole

3 or 4 slices bacon
1/2 cup chopped onion
1 green pepper, chopped
3 tablespoons bacon fat
18 okra pods, sliced
2 fresh tomatoes, sliced, or 1 cup canned, undrained
1 cup fresh corn (or canned corn niblets)
1/2 teaspoon salt

In large skillet fry 3 or 4 slices bacon. Reserve 3 tablespoons bacon fat and let it remain in skillet. Crumble bacon. In skillet sauté onion and pepper. Return crumbled bacon to skillet. Add sliced okra pods, tomatoes, corn, and salt. Simmer covered for 15 minutes.

What to do with all those cucumbers? Salad-making is obvious, but beyond that? Fry them, of course.

Fried Cucumbers

4 medium cucumbers, washed, peeled, and sliced
　crosswise in thin slices
2 eggs, beaten
1 cup milk

1 cup all-purpose flour
1 cup cornmeal
1 teaspoon salt
1/2 teaspoon pepper
canola oil

Wash, peel, and slice fresh cucumbers. A few at a time, dip cucumber slices in a mixture of beaten eggs combined with milk. Place flour and corn meal in a clear plastic zip bag; add salt and pepper. Into bag place cucumbers that have been dipped in egg-milk mixture. In skillet heat about 1-inch oil. Fry coated cucumbers in hot oil. Fry as you would fried green tomatoes.

We first had these for lunch on a snowy winter day in Texas. They were a refreshing break from usual lunch fare.

Garden Stuffed Cheesy Baked Potatoes

4 russet potatoes
2 tablespoons butter
1 small onion, chopped
3/4 cup chopped fresh broccoli crowns
1/2 cup fat free or lite ranch salad dressing
1 cup Cheddar cheese, grated
1 tablespoon oil
salt and pepper to taste

Preheat oven to 425 degrees. Microwave pierced potatoes on high for 12 minutes. Slice off potato tops. Scoop out pulp and keep skins intact. In a medium bowl mash pulp. Heat a small skillet over medium heat; add butter. Add onion and sauté until tender, about 5 minutes. Add onion, broccoli, salad dressing, and cheese to potato pulp; mix well. Brush outside of potato skin shells with oil. Spoon potato mixture into shells. Place on baking sheet. Bake potatoes until heated through, about 15 minutes. Sprinkle with salt and pepper to taste. You also may add fresh parsley and turkey bacon bits on top.

Years after his mother was gone from this earth, my husband was begging for repeats of her famous Breaded Tomatoes recipe. He could (and did) eat this vegetable dish for breakfast. Grandmother Moore was known for adding a surplus of sugar to any vegetable recipe. Goodness knows how many teaspoons her "dash" of sugar actually consisted of, but assuredly just a dash makes it plenty sweet.

Breaded Tomatoes

4 whole tomatoes (or 1 14 1/2-ounce can whole tomatoes)
1/2 cup water
3 slices day-old bread
salt and pepper to taste
dash sugar
1 pinch baking soda

In saucepan add 4 diced tomatoes that have been mashed up so that the juice emerges in pan. Cover with 1/2 cup water. Allow this mixture to come to a boil. Break up the bread slices into pieces and stir into the tomato mixture. Add salt, pepper, sugar, and baking soda. Allow to boil until mixture is thick; simmer for 10 minutes. Serves 4.

Carrot "Pie" is a vegetable side dish, but it's so sweet, you'll think it's dessert. I've made this for many a covered-dish party, especially at Christmas. It disappears quickly; I always bring home an empty dish from a potluck meal. This recipe is delicious either way—with or without the actual pie crust.

Carrot "Pie"

1 pound carrots, peeled, sliced, and boiled, or steamed until tender
1/2 cup melted butter
3 eggs
1 cup sugar
3 tablespoons all-purpose flour
1 teaspoon baking powder
1 teaspoon vanilla

Drain carrots after you cook them; mash thoroughly or blend in blender. Add melted butter. Combine with remaining ingredients. Pour into unbaked pie shell or, to make a crustless pie, into a greased 9-by-9-inch pan. Bake at 350 degrees for 35-40 minutes. Makes 6 servings.

Here's another way we used our vast surplus of cabbage one summer when our garden was riotous with cabbage heads.

Stir-Fried Cabbage

2 cups cabbage, shaved or sliced
1/2 onion, thinly sliced
1 red or green bell pepper, thinly sliced
1 or 2 potatoes, thinly sliced
1 teaspoon soy sauce
salt and pepper to taste
2 tablespoons oil
1 or 2 tablespoons water

In a deep skillet heat oil over medium heat. Add cabbage, peppers, onion, potatoes, and soy sauce. Stir frequently. Add salt and pepper.

You may need to add 1 or 2 tablespoons of water. No liquid remains when done.

Louis made this delicious Eggplant Casserole for our contribution to Yvonne's covered-dish Christmas luncheon for her and Wheat's combined party, usually held on a Sunday before Christmas. Since I was busy making candy the day before, Louis offered to whip this casserole up to help me out in the kitchen. The dish was well-received.

Eggplant Casserole

1 large or 2 medium eggplant
1 small onion, finely chopped
1 tablespoon butter
1/2 cup cream of mushroom soup
1/2 cup mayonnaise
1 cup grated sharp Cheddar cheese
1 egg, beaten
1 cup cracker crumbs
4 tablespoons butter

Peel and cube eggplant. Place in a small amount of salted water. Boil until tender; drain. Do not overcook. Sauté onions in 1 tablespoon butter. Mix onions and other ingredients except cracker crumbs and 2 tablespoons butter. Add eggplant. Mix well. Pour into a 13-by-9-inch baking dish. Melt 2 tablespoons butter and stir into cracker crumbs. Sprinkle over eggplant mixture. Bake at 350 degrees for about 20 minutes.

Yvonne furnished this Mixed Vegetable Casserole recipe because she said she had enjoyed it at several church covered-dish luncheons. You are talking about some outtasight good cooks if you are talking about a church event in Cooper, so you have to know this is a good dish.

Mixed Vegetable Casserole

2 (15-ounce) cans mixed vegetables (tested with Veg-All) or 4-5 cups mixed chopped garden vegetables such as carrots, green beans, green peas, and corn
1 cup celery
1 cup grated Cheddar cheese
1 cup water chestnuts, chopped
1 (15 1/4-ounce) can whole-kernel corn
1 large onion, chopped
1 cup mayonnaise
1 cup sour cream
1 sleeve crackers (tested with Ritz Crackers)
1/2 cup melted butter

Mix vegetables, celery, cheese, water chestnuts, corn, and onion and spread in greased 11-by-7-inch baking dish. Mix mayonnaise and sour cream. Spread on top of vegetable mixture. Crush crackers and mix with melted butter. Sprinkle on top of mixture. Bake at 325 degrees for 30-35 minutes. Serves 6-8.

Another one from Yvonne—Hominy Casserole. This calls for canned yellow hominy, but hominy from the garden would make it even more delightful.

Hominy Casserole

3 (16-ounce) cans yellow hominy, drained, or fresh hominy from the garden
1 (10 1/2-ounce) can cream of mushroom soup
1 small jar chopped pimientos

1 small onion, chopped
1 bell pepper, chopped
1 cup grated Cheddar cheese

Mix all ingredients. Bake in 11-by-7-inch greased casserole at 350 degrees for 40 minutes. Put 1/4 cup grated Cheddar cheese on top. Bake 15 minutes more.

Lynda and George bought some greens at a farmers' market. Lynda had not considered herself a big "greens-eater", but they looked up an online recipe, tried them and became fans.

Southern-Style Greens

2 pounds greens (turnip greens, collard greens, or mustard greens)
6-7 quarts water
1 ham hock or 4-ounce piece of salt pork
1 tablespoon salt

Thoroughly wash greens. Two or more washings may be necessary. Trim tough stalks and tear or cut large greens in pieces. Cut thick veins out of collard greens. In large pot bring the 6-7 quarts of water to a boil. Add the ham hock or salt pork. Add salt. Continue boiling for 10-15 minutes. Add the washed greens to the pot. Cover and simmer until greens are tender. Depending on the type of greens used, this might take an hour. Makes enough for 4 people. Variations/additions: crushed red pepper, a few tablespoons of bacon grease, chopped onion, or other seasonings can be added to the pot for more flavorful greens. Serve with corn bread and pepper sauce or cider vinegar. If desired serve with chopped hard-boiled eggs, bacon pieces, or sliced green onion for garnish.

Jana's Picante Sauce makes 10 pints and has an alternate suggestion for a milder sauce.

Picante Sauce

5 quarts tomatoes, diced
5 cups onion, chopped
18 hot peppers (12-15 for milder sauce)
1 cup vinegar
2/3 cup sugar
8 teaspoons un-iodized salt
6 teaspoons garlic salt

Mix all ingredients together. Bring to a rolling boil for 30 minutes. Seal in hot jars immediately. Makes 10 pints.

One summer we had more tomatoes than we had hairs on the head. This recipe for homemade Tomato Sauce made a product that was so fresh, made you wonder why you'd ever buy canned.

Tomato Sauce

18 tomatoes
2 green peppers
2 onions
3 tablespoons artificial sweetener
2 teaspoons salt
1 teaspoon ground cinnamon
1/2 teaspoon ground cloves
1 teaspoon allspice
2 cups vinegar

Peel, core, and chop tomatoes. Chop pepper and onion. Combine all ingredients. Boil 4 hours until mixture is thick. While mixture is still boiling hot, fill pint jars to within 1/2-inch of jar opening. Process 10 minutes in boiling water bath.

Shelley's Hot Sauce can use fresh tomatoes and chilies or can be subbed with canned.

Hot Sauce

    chopped onion to taste
    1 (7-ounce) can green chilies (or fresh chilies)
    jalapeño to taste
    1 lime
    1 teaspoon garlic or 1-2 cloves
    1 teaspoon salt
    2 (14 1/2-ounce) cans Mexican stewed tomatoes
    1 cup diced tomato with cilantro (or use 1 cup fresh
        tomato with several sprigs of cilantro added)
    1/8 cup sugar

Blend onion with 2 tablespoons green chilies and 2 tablespoons jalapeño. Add lime juice from 1 lime, sugar, garlic, green chilies, salt, and tomatoes. Process in blender.

Parslied Potatoes make a wonderful side dish with meat loaf, chicken, steaks, or whatever. I love redskin potatoes but struggle for ways to make them less boring. This recipe definitely adds some life to this dish.

Parslied Potatoes

    1 1/2 pounds small, new red potatoes, scrubbed
    1 tablespoon oil
    1 medium onion, chopped
    1 small clove garlic, crushed

1 cup low-sodium chicken broth
1 cup chopped fresh parsley, divided
1/2 teaspoon pepper

Peel a strip of skin from around the middle of each potato; place potatoes in cold water. Set aside. Heat a large skillet over medium-high heat. Add oil. Sauté onion and garlic for 5 minutes or until tender. Add broth and 3/4 cup parsley; mix well. Bring to a boil. Place potatoes in a single layer in skillet. Avoid overcrowding. Return to a boil; reduce heat. Simmer, covered, for 10-15 minutes or until potatoes are tender when you test with fork. Remove potatoes with a slotted spoon to serving bowl. Add pepper to skillet; stir. Pour sauce over potatoes. Sprinkle with remaining parsley.

Louis' mother had been a noted cook of Baked Apples, so I wanted to be sure I pleased my hubby in this regard. Food Editor Ann Criswell, who worked in the cubicle next to me at the *Houston Chronicle*, knew of my plight and shared this recipe with me.

Baked Apples

4 baking apples
1/2 cup water
1/4 cup honey
1 teaspoon grated lemon or orange rind

Preheat oven to 375 degrees. Wash and core apples; place in baking dish. Combine the honey with the water and grated rind. Pour over the apples and bake, covered, for 30 minutes, basting two or three times. Uncover, baste again, and bake 15 minutes longer or until tender. Makes 4 servings.

I can't even begin to describe how much I learned from being an officemate of Ann Criswell, who was nationally and even internationally known for her years of writing on foods. Few people are as blessed as I was to have a mentor of her caliber. Here is another of her favorites that she passed on to me. This food item will knock the socks off other guests when you take it to a bring-a-dish gathering.

Green Beans Supreme

  1/2 cup sliced onion
  1 tablespoon parsley
  4 tablespoons butter
  2 tablespoons all-purpose flour
  1 teaspoon salt
  1/4 teaspoon pepper
  1/2 teaspoon lemon juice
  1 cup sour cream
  5 cups cooked fresh green beans
  1/2 cup grated Cheddar cheese
  1/2 cup dried bread crumbs

Sauté onions and parsley in 2 tablespoons butter until tender. Add flour, salt, pepper, and lemon juice, stirring. Add sour cream, then beans. Heat but do not boil. Turn into 2-quart dish. Top with grated cheese. Sprinkle crumbs and remaining butter over beans. Broil at low heat until cheese melts and crumbs brown.

I found this recipe after one of our trips to the Chickasaw farmers' market.

Creamed Turnip Greens

  1 1/2 pounds turnip greens, cleaned and stripped of
    their skins

1 tablespoon butter
1/2 cup minced onions
1 cup chicken broth
1 tablespoon all-purpose flour
1/2 cup milk
1/4 to 1/2 cup heavy cream
salt and pepper to taste

Drop cleaned leaves into large pot of boiling water. Return to boil. Drain leaves and chop fine. Melt butter in skillet. Add onions and cook until just soft. Add greens and broth. Simmer, partly covered, until greens are tender, 20-25 minutes. Uncover and stir over high heat until moisture evaporates. Sprinkle in flour and stir 2 minutes. Add milk and 1/4 cup cream. Simmer; stir. Cover and cook on low heat. Add cream and salt and pepper to taste. Simmer for an additional 5-10 minutes.

Louis and I will never dine on turnips without remembering the summer of 1971 when we returned to Texas for me to finish my Baylor degree. We lived on love and a Spartan food budget. To stretch our food dollar until it screamed, we bought a lot of turnips (very inexpensive) and made a serving last an entire week. In later life, when our food budget had a bit more "give" to it, we laughed as we doctored up turnips in the following fashion and remember the days of deep, deep frugality, which were highly instructional for us.

Turnip and Onion Gratin

1/2 pound turnips, peeled and grated
1 onion, chopped fine
2 teaspoons cornstarch
1 1/4 cups plus 1 tablespoon finely grated
   Parmesan cheese

salt and pepper
1/3 cup heavy cream

In a bowl toss the turnips and the onion with the cornstarch, 1/4 cup Parmesan, and salt and pepper to taste. Transfer the mixture to a buttered 9-inch square dish. Pat down mixture. Drizzle the cream evenly over mixture. Sprinkle it with remaining 1 tablespoon Parmesan. Bake at 375 degrees for 25-30 minutes.

One summer day in our early marriage Louis and I stopped by Aunt Bonnie and Uncle Bill's country home for a visit near a mealtime. Aunt Bonnie had just brought in some fresh ears of corn from her marvelous garden; she prepared for us this recipe for Fried Corn. Louis extolled this to the sky; he had never dined on something so close to perfection. Aunt Bonnie, in her ever-gracious way, wrote down the recipe for him. A host of summers later, Louis could still feel his tastebuds spring alive at the mere thought of this dish.

Fried Corn

8 ears fresh corn
1/2 cup milk
1/2 teaspoon salt
1/4 teaspoon pepper
4 tablespoons butter
2 eggs

Cut corn from cob and add milk, salt, and pepper. Put butter in a heavy skillet. When skillet is hot, add corn. Cook until tender. Stir occasionally. Just before corn is ready to take up, add beaten eggs and blend in well.

The mixture of fresh corn and broccoli, along with a can of creamed corn, make Savory Corn and Broccoli a delightful side dish.

Savory Corn and Broccoli

Corn kernels from 1 1/2 ears fresh corn on the cob, or 1 (11-ounce) can whole-kernel corn, no salt added, drained
1 (14 3/4-ounce) can cream-style golden sweet corn, no salt added, drained
1 1/2 cups small broccoli florets
1/4 cup sliced green onion
2 tablespoons all-purpose flour
1 egg, beaten (or 2 egg whites)
1/4 teaspoon pepper
1/4 cup (about 6 wafers) crushed low-salt shredded wheat wafers

Steam corn for 4 minutes in microwave. Cut kernels from cob. Set aside. In medium bowl stir together cream corn and flour until combined. Stir in fresh (or canned whole-kernel) corn, broccoli, onions, egg, and pepper. Spray 9-inch pie plate with cooking spray. Spoon mixture into pie plate. Sprinkle with crushed wavers. Bake at 350 degrees for 30-35 minutes or until set.

Eleene furnished this Southwestern-Style Succotash recipe that appears on the next page. She says you can add one 4-ounce can chopped green jalapeños if you want to "add a little fire" to it.

Southwestern-Style Succotash

3 strips smoked bacon
1 diced green pepper
1 diced red pepper
1 medium diced onion
2 (15 1/4-ounce) cans whole-kernel corn, drained (or use fresh corn kernels cut from the cob)
2 (16-ounce) cans green lima beans, drained
1 (14-ounce) can chicken broth
1 cup water
1 (4-ounce) can mild, chopped green chilies
salt and pepper to taste

Cook bacon in a large kettle until the bacon is crisp; then remove to a paper towel. Add green and red peppers and onions to bacon drippings in pot and sauté until tender. Crumble the two cooked bacon slices into small pieces and add to pot along with the corn, lima beans, chicken broth, water, chilies, and salt and pepper. Bring to boil and cook for five minutes. Then simmer for 20 minutes or until liquid is reduced as desired

When Katie and Casey married, Casey's family friend Deborah Davies compiled for them a loose-leaf notebook filled with Davies family recipes. Katie cooks from this often (See what I mean? People enjoy knowing what recipes are tried-and-true in someone else's family.) and especially enjoys Deborah's recipe for Glazed Carrots.

Glazed Carrots

1 1/2 pounds fresh carrots
1/3 cup brown sugar, packed

1/2 teaspoon salt
1/2 teaspoon grated orange peel
2 tablespoons butter

Prepare and cook carrots. Cut into lengthwise strips. Cover and boil 18-20 minutes in 1 inch of salted water. In large skillet cook and stir brown sugar, salt, orange peel, and butter until mixture is bubbly. Add carrot strips; cook over low heat. Stir occasionally about 5 minutes or until carrots are glazed and heated through. Makes 6 servings.

Casey's mom, Debbie Welch, gave me this recipe for Zucchini Au Gratin—a favorite at the Welch home.

Zucchini Au Gratin

1/4 cup butter
3-4 large zucchini, sliced
garlic salt, dried onion, mixed seasonings (tested with
    Nature's Seasonings)
4 ounces cheese spread (tested with Velveeta)
large handful shredded Cheddar cheese
1/2 cup milk
1/4 cup bread crumbs
1 cup French-fried onions
1/2 cup sour cream

In skillet melt butter; add zucchini. Season to taste with garlic salt, dried onion, and mixed seasonings. Sauté until slightly tender. Remove zucchini from skillet and place in greased 7-by-11-inch casserole dish.In skillet melt cheeses; add sour cream and milk, bread crumbs, and half of the French-fried onions Mix until texture is creamy. If more milk is needed, add it at this time. Pour mixture over zucchini. Top with remaining French-fried onions. Bake at 350 until mixture is bubbly—about 20 minutes. Makes about 6 servings.

Main Dishes

When our garden begins to have its annual profusion of green peppers, we chop and freeze them in plastic storage containers so we'll have plenty of green peppers on hand for winter recipes. We also make up batches of Stuffed Green Peppers and freeze these to have available for fall and winter entrees. When we can do so, we like to have a freezer full of what we call "December entrees", so meals during the frantic month of December are ready to thaw and pop into the microwave for busy nights. Here's the recipe for Stuffed Green Peppers I've prepared ever since I was a new bride.

Stuffed Green Peppers

3 large green peppers
1 cup boiling salted water
1/2 pound ground beef or ground turkey
1 (8-ounce) can tomato sauce
1/2 cup coarse dry bread crumbs or cracker crumbs
1 teaspoon salt
1/4 teaspoon pepper
1 tablespoon chopped onion

Cut a thin slice from the stem end of each green pepper. Wash outside and inside. Remove all seeds and membranes. Cook peppers in boiling salted water for 5 minutes. Drain. Mix rest of ingredients. Stuff peppers lightly with mixture. Stand upright in small baking dish. Bake covered at 350 degrees for 45 minutes; uncover and bake 15 minutes more. Makes 2-3 servings. (Double or triple recipe if preparing to serve larger numbers.)

My husband is obsessed with finding summertime entrees that don't heat up the kitchen by requiring oven usage. We love these Vegetable Quesadillas (after Casey joined the family we began calling them *Casey-dillas*) because they call for fresh garden produce and are made on the stovetop—an ideal light, summer meal—blazin' good!

Vegetable Quesadillas

   2 tablespoons olive oil
   1 large green pepper, cored and chopped
   8 ounces sliced mushrooms
   1/8 teaspoon salt
   1/8 teaspoon pepper
   8 fajita-size flour tortillas (7-inch diameter)
   1 1/3 cups shredded pepperjack cheese
   2 medium ears corn, steamed and cut from cob,
       enough to make 1 1/4 cups fresh corn kernels.
       May substitute 1 (11-ounce) can Mexicorn

In a large, nonstick skillet heat 2 tablespoons olive oil. Add green pepper, mushrooms, salt, and pepper. Sauté over medium-high heat for 5 minutes or until green pepper softens. Stir occasionally. Remove from heat. Place flour tortillas on a flat work surface. Place about 1/3 cup pepper-and-mushroom mixture over each. Divide evenly. Sprinkle 1/3 cup cheese over each tortilla. Top each with another tortilla. Wipe out skillet; coat with nonstick cooking spray and heat over medium-high heat. Place 1 quesadilla in the skillet. Cook 2 minutes. Gently press down with a spatula. Turn and cook an additional 1 to 2 minutes, until quesadilla is lightly browned and cheese melts. Remove from skillet. Keep quesadillas warm. Repeat process with remaining quesadillas. To serve, heat corn. Cut each quesadilla into wedges and serve with the corn. Serves 4.

One of our all-time faves (another good light summer entree) is this recipe for Cabbage Sloppy Joes—a great, tasty way to use cabbage as well as garden green pepper and onions. In case the idea of cabbage in a sloppy-joe recipe gets a *yuk* response, the cabbage is almost indistinguishable and adds a sweet taste to the end-product.

Cabbage Sloppy Joes

1 pound ground beef or ground turkey
1 1/2 cups finely shredded cabbage
1 medium onion, chopped
1 celery rib, chopped
1/4 cup chopped green pepper
1 cup ketchup (we use the no-salt variety)
3 tablespoons brown sugar
2 tablespoons lemon juice
1 tablespoon vinegar
1 tablespoon Worcestershire sauce
1 tablespoon prepared mustard
1 teaspoon salt
dash pepper
8 sandwich rolls, split

In a large skillet cook the ground beef (or turkey), cabbage, onion, celery, and green pepper over medium heat until meat no longer is pink and vegetables are crisp-tender. Drain. Stir in the ketchup, brown sugar, lemon juice, vinegar, Worcestershire sauce, mustard, salt, and pepper. Cover and simmer for 10 minutes or until cabbage is tender. Spoon 1/2 cup onto each roll. Makes 8 servings.

Squash, zucchini, and tomatoes from the garden all find a home in this delicious Zucchini and Tomato Galette, which is like a vegetarian pizza. Alongside a small bowl of fresh cut-up fruit this dish makes a delightful, easy meal.

Zucchini and Tomato Galette

2 yellow squash, sliced lengthwise
2 medium zucchini, sliced lengthwise
1 1/2 teaspoons olive oil
1/4 teaspoon salt
1 refrigerated piecrust (or your favorite homemade piecrust)
1/3 cup finely grated Parmesan cheese
1/4 cup bread crumbs
2 tablespoons chopped basil
4 small-to-medium-sized tomatoes, sliced
1 egg white, beaten

Heat a countertop grill or outdoor grill. In large bowl toss yellow squash and zucchini slices with oil and salt. Grill vegetables, turning once, until cooked through, about 10 minutes. Let cool. Heat oven to 400 degrees. On lightly floured surface roll piecrust into 14-inch circle. Carefully transfer to baking sheet. In small bowl combine cheese, bread crumbs, and basil; spread mixture in 9-inch circle in middle of piecrust. Arrange half of the grilled squash slices in spoke fashion to cover cheese mixture. Place tomato slices over squash; arrange remaining squash slices over tomatoes. Fold outer edge of dough over vegetables to make top layer of crust. Brush top of crust with beaten egg white. Bake 30 minutes or until crust is golden brown. Serve warm or at room temperature. Makes 6 servings.

Cabbage Rolls, featured on the next page, was a favorite dish of Aunt Frances. She was first served Cabbage Rolls at a Sunday-school class covered-dish dinner.

Cabbage Rolls

8 cabbage leaves
1/2 cup long-grain rice
1 cup water
1/2 teaspoon salt
1 pound ground beef (or ground turkey)
1 tablespoon finely chopped onion
1 (1/2-ounce) envelope spaghetti-sauce mix
1 (1-pound) can whole tomatoes, undrained
1/4 cup evaporated milk, undiluted

Steam cabbage leaves in water for 8 minutes or until they are slightly softened; drain thoroughly. Combine rice, water, and salt; cook 20 minutes or until tender. Mix together rice, beef, onion, and 1 tablespoon spaghetti-sauce mix. Fill each leaf with approximately 1/3 cup meat mix. Fold leaf over meat; tuck in ends; fasten with toothpicks. Place rolls with overlapped side down in large skillet that has been sprayed with cooking spray. Mix together tomatoes and remaining contents of sauce-mix envelope; pour over cabbage. Simmer covered for 1 hour. Place rolls on platter; remove toothpicks. To tomato liquid in pan add evaporated milk. Simmer until thickened but do not boil. Serve cabbage rolls steaming hot with sauce. Makes 4 servings.

I found this Zucchini Quiche recipe in a magazine designed to help people who want to abandon big-city life and take up country living. The recipe section was to help people who found they had harvested enough of this prolific vegetable to have it for breakfast, lunch, and dinner.

Zucchini Quiche

4 cups shredded zucchini
3 eggs
1/2 cup oil
1/2 cup grated Parmesan cheese
1 small onion, finely chopped
3 strips of bacon, fried and crumbled
1 cup boxed baking mix (tested with Bisquick)

Combine all ingredients and place in a greased pie pan. Bake at 350 degrees for 45 minutes. Makes 6 servings.

The following Southwest Mini Quiche recipe was provided by the Chickasaw Nation Nutrition Services. This office gives Chickasaw citizens cooking tips on how to prepare the fresh vegetables provided them at the roadside stands in Oklahoma. I fixed this delightful, easy recipe for Louis and me the very next day after we visited the Chickasaw Nation and I got this recipe card.

Southwest Mini Quiche

1 boneless, skinless chicken breast, cooked and shredded
1 tablespoon taco seasoning (buy packaged taco seasoning and use 1 tablespoon of it)
1 1/4 cups egg substitute
3 tablespoons chopped green bell peppers
2 tablespoons chopped onion
1/2 cup corn, fresh or frozen/thawed
3 tablespoons skim milk
6 corn tortillas
1/2 cup water
1 cup Cheddar cheese, reduced fat

Spray 12-cup muffin pan with nonstick cooking spray. Quarter the tortillas and place 2 quarters into each muffin cup so that the tortilla pieces fan out to fill the cup. To a small pan add chicken, water, and 1 tablespoon of taco seasoning. Bring water to a boil, then immediately lower heat and allow to cook down until water evaporates. Place a spoonful of chicken in each tortilla cup. In a small bowl mix egg substitute, onions, peppers, corn, and milk. Pour a scant 1/4 cup of egg mixture over chicken. Top each cup with cheese and bake at 350 degrees for 25 minutes. Makes 12 mini quiches.

We visited Matthew and Marcie in Phoenix to celebrate a late Christmas 2009 just before our grandson Ryan was born. We wanted to make sure Marcie could rest, so I prepared this recipe, which others proclaimed as delicious. Addition of carrots and other garden-fresh vegetables are a real plus.

Thick and Chunky Tomato Spaghetti Sauce

1 pound ground turkey
1 large onion, finely chopped
1/2 cup celery, finely chopped
2 teaspoons garlic powder
1/4 cup olive oil
1 (16-ounce) can tomato sauce
4 cups fresh tomatoes, diced (can substitute 2
    14 1/2-ounce cans diced tomatoes)
1/2 tablespoon oregano
1/2 tablespoon basil
1 tablespoon parsley
1/4 teaspoon salt
1 tablespoon sugar
1 (6-ounce) can tomato paste
1/2 cup fresh mushrooms, chopped
1 medium carrot, grated
1/2 cup black olives, chopped

In large pot brown ground turkey, celery, and onion. Drain. Add remaining ingredients. Bring to a boil. Lower heat and simmer for three hours. Serve over pasta. This sauce also can be cooled and frozen in freezer bags.

During our Nashville years I was pleased to be part of the LifeWay team that introduced to churches the *First Place* Christ-centered health program. This recipe for Pork Chops and Apples was one of my favorites from the *First Place* recipe book.

Pork Chops with Apples

>4 lean center-cut pork chops
>1 medium onion, chopped
>1 1/4 cups water
>1 teaspoon low-sodium chicken-flavored bouillon granules
>1/4 teaspoon pepper
>3 apples, peeled and sliced
>1/2 teaspoon ground cinnamon

In skillet brown pork chops and onion. In glass measuring cup combine water, bouillon granules, and pepper. Stir to dissolve; add to skillet. Cover and bring to boil. Reduce heat and simmer 20 minutes. Add apple slices and cinnamon. Cover and simmer 15 more minutes. Serves 4.

This Chunky Chili is another recipe we prepared for the Arizona Moore family in the time just before baby Ryan arrived. It's healthy with fresh vegetables added to the usual chili mixture. Just marvelous!

Chunky Chili

1 pound ground turkey
2 garlic cloves, crushed (or 2 teaspoons garlic powder)
1 small onion, coarsely chopped
1 each large red and green bell peppers, coarsely chopped
1 cup butternut squash, peeled and coarsely chopped
2 cups fresh corn kernels, removed from cob (or
   1 (10-ounce) package frozen corn
3 cups tomatoes, diced (or 2 14-ounce cans diced tomatoes)
1 (15-ounce) can chili beans
1 (14-ounce) can beef broth (or 2 cups beef broth made from
   low-sodium beef bouillon granules)
1 1/2 teaspoons chili powder
1 teaspoon ground cumin

In a Dutch oven or large pot, brown the ground turkey. Stir until crumbly; drain. Add the garlic, onion, bell peppers, and squash and mix well. Stir in corn, tomatoes, beans, broth, chili powder, and cumin. Simmer for 30 minutes. Serves 8.

This Spinach and Mushroom Frittata is a great, healthy entree dish. It is especially good served with salsa.

Spinach and Mushroom Frittata

1 stick butter
2 cups mushrooms, thinly sliced
1/4 cup green onions, chopped
2 tablespoons fresh parsley, chopped
2 tablespoons fresh garlic, chopped
1 package (5 ounces) fresh spinach
12 eggs beaten (or 3 cups egg substitute)
1/4 cup Parmesan cheese, grated
3/4 cup skim or 2-percent milk

1/2 teaspoon salt
1/2 teaspoon pepper

In small skillet sauté mushrooms and onions in the butter. Add parsley, garlic, and spinach. Sauté until most of the liquid evaporates. Remove from heat. Add milk and Parmesan to beaten eggs. Add remaining ingredients. Spray 9-inch round glass dish with nonstick cooking spray. Pour in egg mixture. Bake at 350 degrees for 45 minutes or until set in the middle. Refrigerate any leftovers. Serves 6.

Just delicious! No other way to describe this tasty recipe, made special (we thought) by the addition of the turkey bacon. This was Sunday lunch for Louis and me on the day before Ryan was born in Arizona.

Zesty Penne and Broccoli

2 1/2 cups fresh broccoli (or 1 24-ounce package fresh broccoli florets)
1 pound whole-grain penne pasta, cooked and drained
1/2 cup Italian dressing
1/4 cup pimientos, chopped
1 teaspoon pepper
6 slices turkey bacon, cooked crisp and crumbled

Place broccoli in a saucepan and cover with water. Place on stove top and bring to a boil. Boil for 3 minutes, or until tender, and then drain. In large bowl combine cooked broccoli, penne pasta, dressing, pimientos, and pepper. Top with crumbled bacon and serve. Refrigerate any leftovers. Serves 8.

Soft Tacos with Southwestern Vegetables is another idea furnished by the Chickasaw Nation Nutrition Services. My appreciative hubby kept extolling, "This is just marvelous! This is just marvelous!"

Soft Tacos with Southwestern Vegetables

1 tablespoon olive oil
1 medium red onion, chopped
1 cup yellow summer squash, diced
1 cup zucchini, diced
3 large garlic cloves, minced
4 medium tomatoes, seeded and chopped
1 jalapeño, seeded and chopped
kernels from 1 corn cob, steamed and removed from cob, or
    1 cup frozen corn
1 cup canned black beans, rinsed and drained
1/4 cup fresh cilantro, chopped
12 corn tortillas

In a large saucepan heat the olive oil over medium heat. Add the onion and cook until soft. Add the squash and zucchini and continue cooking until tender, about 5 minutes. Stir in the garlic, tomatoes, jalapeño, corn, and beans. Cook until the vegetables are crisp-tender, about 5 minutes. Add the cilantro and remove from heat. Heat a dry, large frying pan (without a nonstick surface) over medium heat. Add 1 tortilla to the hot pan and heat until softened, about 20 seconds per side. Repeat with the remaining tortillas. Stuff veggie mixture into warmed tortillas. Serve salsa and sour cream on the side.

What a treasure we added to our family when Jarod married Cara! She is a talented, precious person and is admired by all. She furnished this Zucchini Pizza Casserole recipe which she says her mother prepared when Cara was growing up. Her mom even grew the zucchini in her own garden.

Zucchini Pizza Casserole

1/2 teaspoon lemon pepper
1/2 teaspoon garlic salt
1/3 cup olive oil
6-8 medium zucchini
1/3 cup chopped onion
1/3 cup chopped green pepper
1/3 cup sliced fresh mushrooms
1 cup chopped fresh tomatoes
1 (3.8-ounce) can chopped black olives
sliced pepperoni
mozzarella cheese

Slice zucchini in 1/2-inch slices. Toss sliced zucchini in olive oil, lemon pepper, and garlic. Lay half of the sliced zucchini in the bottom of a greased 10-by-10-inch casserole dish. Chop mushrooms and mix with onions, green peppers, and tomatoes. Layer half of mixture on top of the zucchini in the dish. Repeat the layers with the remainder of zucchini and veggie mixture. Top with your preferred amount of pepperoni. Bake at 350 degrees for 30 minutes. Top casserole with cheese and then bake until the cheese is melted.

On the subject of zucchini, we added this recipe for Asian Chicken with Zucchini when we added Casey to the family. Katie says it's a winner with her, especially because it gets Casey in the kitchen to be the chef.

Casey's Asian Chicken with Zucchini

2-3 skinless, boneless chicken breasts
3 bell peppers (1 red, 1 yellow, 1 orange)
1 medium zucchini

    1 teaspoon minced garlic
    2 tablespoons soy sauce
    1 tablespoon olive oil
    spaghetti, your choice

Slice bell peppers and zucchini into julienne-type strips. Cut chicken into thin slices. Set aside. In large skillet over medium-high heat, add olive oil and minced garlic. Sauté garlic until it is golden. Reduce heat. Add bell peppers and zucchini. Allow vegetables to cook until fork-tender. Move vegetables to side of skillet. Add sliced chicken. Cover. Periodically stir chicken. In separate pot, boil spaghetti until it reaches *al dente* texture. Once chicken is fully cooked, add 2 tablespoons soy sauce to saucepan. Mix chicken, soy sauce, and vegetables. Reduce heat and cover. Once spaghetti is cooked and drained, add to chicken-vegetable mixture. If needed for flavor, add 2 tablespoons additional soy sauce.

    Calico Beef Burgers is another main dish we served during that historic visit in 1979 when members of my birthfamily visited us in Houston for the first time.

Calico Beef Burgers

    3/4 pound ground beef or ground turkey
    1 cup cold cooked potatoes, riced or mashed
    1/2 cup shredded carrot
    1/4 cup finely chopped green onion
    1/4 cup grated Parmesan cheese
    1 egg
    1 tablespoon steak sauce
    1/2 teaspoon salt
    1/8 teaspoon pepper

Combine ingredients; shape into patties, grill burgers. Serve on toasted buns or patties by themselves without the buns.

Desserts

This Fresh Apple Cake recipe made its debut in my *Way Back in the Country* cookbook. My mother baked it each Christmas for years on end. The strawberry and apricot preserves make it moist. It keeps for many days.

Fresh Apple Cake

4 apples, peeled and chopped
2 cups sugar
1 cup oil
2 eggs
3 cups all-purpose flour
1 cup chopped nuts
1/2 cup strawberry preserves
1/2 cup apricot preserves
2 teaspoons soda
1/2 teaspoon salt
2 teaspoons vanilla
1 teaspoon cinnamon
1/2 teaspoon allspice
1/4 teaspoon nutmeg

In a large bowl, place chopped apples; add sugar and let stand 20 minutes. Add oil and eggs. Then add all other ingredients. Bake in a greased and floured tube or Bundt pan at 300 degrees for 1 1/2 hours.

This recipe for Brown Sugar Apple Pie was one of the treasures I found in Aunt Frances' recipe box after she passed away.

Brown Sugar Apple Pie

1 unbaked pie crust
6-7 tart apples, peeled and sliced
1/3 cup brown sugar
2 tablespoons quick-cooking tapioca
2 tablespoons lemon juice
1 teaspoon cinnamon
1/2 teaspoon nutmeg
1/2 cup brown sugar
2/3 cup grated Cheddar cheese
1/2 cup all-purpose flour
1/3 cup butter

In a medium bowl combine apple slices, 1/3 cup brown sugar, tapioca, lemon juice, cinnamon, and nutmeg. Stir well. Arrange in pastry shell. In small bowl mix 1/2 cup brown sugar, grated cheese, and flour. Using pastry blender or two knives, cut in butter. Sprinkle over apple mixture. Bake at 425 degrees for 40-45 minutes or until apples are tender. Serve warm with wedges of cheese. Serves 6.

My mother's specialty—Spiced Sugared Pecans—tastes like Christmas. I miss my mom all the time but especially when I dine on these. They *are* her kitchen at Christmastime.

Spiced Sugared Pecans

1/2 cup brown sugar
1 cup sugar
1/3 cup water
1 teaspoon ground cinnamon
1/2 teaspoon nutmeg
1/8 teaspoon salt
1 1/2 cups pecan halves

Mix sugars together and boil in 1/3 cup water until the mixture forms a hard ball in water. Add cinnamon, nutmeg, and salt. Stir in pecan halves. Stir until nuts cling together. Pour out onto waxed paper. Separate into individual pieces or small chunks. Let cool.

Bring on the peach crop for this delicious Fresh Peach Pudding recipe. It's great with or without the whipped topping as a garnish.

Fresh Peach Pudding

   3 eggs
   1 cup sugar
   1 tablespoon all-purpose flour
   1 1/4 cups evaporated milk (not sweetened condensed milk)
   1 teaspoon vanilla
   1 teaspoon almond flavoring
   1 cup peeled, sliced, and chopped peaches
   2 tablespoons butter
   fat-free whipped topping, if desired

Mix eggs, sugar, and flour with evaporated milk; add vanilla and almond flavoring. Melt butter in an 8-by-8-inch pan; pour peaches over butter, then pour batter over peaches and butter. Bake at 300 degrees until firm.

A neighbor's gift of a sack of fresh pears from his farm inspired me to find this Pear Cake recipe that appears on the next page. This cake freezes extremely well.

Pear Cake

3 cups chopped pears
2 cups sugar
1 cup oil
3 cups all-purpose flour
2 eggs
1 teaspoon cinnamon
1 teaspoon ground cloves
1 teaspoon ground allspice
2 teaspoons soda
1 teaspoon salt
1 cup pecans, chopped

Mix first three ingredients; let stand for one hour. Beat eggs and add to pear mixture. Sift all dry ingredients together and add to pear mixture. Add chopped pecans. Pour into greased and floured tube pan or two loaf pans. Bake at 350 degrees for 1 hour.

Fresh apples are not generally found in a cookie recipe, but this one for Harvest Softies features a finely shredded McIntosh apple that helps create a wonderfully soft, cake-like cookie. The icing made with apple juice makes this pretty enough for a party tray. Katie and I served this at a fall baby shower we tossed for Marcie when she was expecting Ryan.

Harvest Softies

Cookies:
1 McIntosh apple, peeled and cored
1/2 cup apple juice
1/2 cup (1 stick) butter, softened
1 cup brown sugar
1 egg

1/4 teaspoon cinnamon
2 1/2 cups self-rising flour

Icing:
1 (16-ounce) box powdered sugar (4 cups)
1/3 cup apple juice

Line 2 large baking sheets with foil. Lightly spray foil so cookies won't stick. Grate apple into a bowl; add apple juice. In a separate large bowl with a mixer beat butter, sugar, egg, and cinnamon until mixture is fluffy, about 2 minutes. With a spoon, stir in half the flour, the apple mixture, then remaining flour. Drop batter by tablespoons onto the prepared sheets, with cookies spaced 3 inches apart. Bake cookies at 350 degrees for 17 minutes until cookies are lightly browned. Remove to a rack; cool completely. Repeat. For icing, in medium-sided bowl blend sifted powdered sugar and apple juice until smooth and firm enough so icing won't run. Spread icing on top of cookie; leave about 1/4 inch of cookie showing around edge. When icing is firm, store cookies in refrigerator until time to serve.

Apple slices in these cookies make them nutritious as well as tasty. This recipe was furnished by the Chickasaw Nation as its nutrition services department endeavors to help Chickasaw people have better lives.

Super Cereal Squares

cooking spray
3 cups multigrain oat circle cereal (such as multigrain Cheerios)
1/2 cup honey
1/4 cup brown sugar
1 cup apple slices, dried, chopped
1/2 teaspoon cinnamon

>   1/2 cup peanut butter
>   2 tablespoons mini chocolate chips

Lightly spray an 8-by-8-inch baking dish. Place cereal in plastic bag and seal. Slightly crush with hands or rolling pin. In saucepan heat honey, brown sugar, apples, and cinnamon on medium-high until it simmers. Remove from heat and add peanut butter. Mix well. Add cereal and stir gently. Press mixture into dish. Sprinkle with chocolate chips that you press into the cookie mixture and refrigerate about 1 hour until set. Cut into 16 squares.

Like the Peach-Plum Crumble recipe featured on page 44, this one for Peach-Blueberry Pie combines two fruits I adore and that many people wouldn't imagine putting together. What a flavor! Smokin' good!

Peach-Blueberry Pie

>   1 cup sugar
>   1/3 cup all-purpose flour
>   1/2 teaspoon ground cinnamon
>   1/8 teaspoon ground allspice
>   3 cups sliced peeled fresh peaches
>   1 cup fresh blueberries
>   1 tablespoon butter
>   pastry for double-crust pie (9 inches)
>   milk
>   cinnamon
>   sugar

In a bowl combine sugar, flour, cinnamon, and allspice. Add the peaches and blueberries; toss gently. Line pie plate with bottom crust; add the filling. Dot with butter. Top with a lattice crust. Brush crust with milk; sprinkle with cinnamon and sugar. Bake at 400 degrees for 40-45 minutes or until crust is golden brown and filing is bubbly. Cool completely. Frozen fruit may be used if it is thawed and well-drained. Serves 6-8.

Speaking of blueberries, this recipe has been with me since our Houston days. I just have to prepare it at least once a summer. To me it represents the pure essence of a summer day.

Deep-Dish Blueberry Pie

    4 cups fresh blueberries
    1 cup sugar plus 2 tablespoons, divided
    1/3 cup all-purpose flour
    1/4 teaspoon salt
    1 tablespoon fresh lemon juice
    1 1/4 cups all-purpose flour
    1 1/2 teaspoons baking powder
    1/4 teaspoon salt
    1/8 teaspoon cardamom or nutmeg
    1/4 cup butter
    1/3 cup milk

To prepare filling in medium bowl mix blueberries, 1 cup sugar, 1/3 cup flour, salt, and lemon juice. Turn into greased 1-quart casserole. To prepare topping mix 1 1/4 cups flour, 2 tablespoons sugar, baking powder, salt, and cardamom in medium bowl. Cut in butter until mixture resembles coarse meal. Add milk and stir just until smooth. Form into ball and roll out on floured surface to a 9-inch circle (or 2 inches larger than the diameter of the casserole). Place over blueberries and seal over edge. Bake at 400 degrees for 40 minutes until topping is browned. Serve warm with ice cream. Makes 6 servings.

I'm a total nut-case for bread puddings. I love them in all varieties. As I grew up, I couldn't imagine why my mother would choose bread pudding in the cafeteria line when so many chocolate-y desserts were available. Now I regard any kind of bread pudding as the dessert of royalty. Here's one that uses delicious fresh apples.

Apple Bread Pudding

    1 teaspoon butter
    2 cups stale bread, cut in 1/2-inch cubes
    2 medium-sized tart unpeeled apples, cored, diced
    2 eggs
    1/2 cup sugar
    2 cups skim or 1-percent milk
    1 teaspoon vanilla extract
    1/2 teaspoon cinnamon

Grease inside of 1 1/2-quart casserole. In a mixing bowl toss bread cubes with diced apples; turn into buttered casserole dish. In same mixing bowl beat eggs until foamy, then beat in sugar, milk, vanilla, and cinnamon; pour over bread and apples. Push bread under to soak up liquid. Bake on middle shelf of 350-degree oven until pudding is slightly puffed and set, 50-60 minutes. Serve warm or cold with purchased caramel sauce.

I've always thought this "upside-down" recipe was novel and another great way to use fresh apples.

Upside-Down Pecan Apple Pie

    1 cup chopped pecans
    1/2 cup brown sugar
    1/3 cup butter, melted
    1 package refrigerated piecrusts, or your favorite 2-crust

piecrust recipe
6 cups apples, thinly sliced
1/4 cup sugar
2 tablespoons all-purpose flour
1/2 teaspoon cinnamon
1/3 teaspoon nutmeg

Combine pecans, brown sugar, and butter in a 9-inch pie pan. Spread evenly over bottom of pan. Place pie crust over pecan mixture. In large bowl combine apples, sugar, flour, cinnamon, and nutmeg. Spoon into crust-lined pan. Top with remaining crust. Fold edge of top crust under bottom crust. Press together to seal. Flute edge. Cut slits in top crust. Bake at 375 degrees for 40-50 minutes. Cover edge of crust with strips of foil after 15-20 minutes of baking to prevent excessive browning. Cool pie upright for 5 minutes. Place serving plate over pie; invert. Carefully remove pan. Cool at least 1 hour before serving.

The *Chronicle*'s Ann Criswell was a resource once again for this carrot-cake recipe that lives up to its name of "Fabulous". One time when I was giving a party with many guests, I made four of these three-layer cakes. I froze the layers in advance, then thawed and frosted them at party time.

Fabulous Carrot Cake

2 cups sugar
2 cups all-purpose flour
2 teaspoons baking soda
2 teaspoons cinnamon
4 eggs, beaten
1 (8-ounce) can crushed pineapple and juice
1 1/2 cups oil
2 teaspoons vanilla

1 teaspoon salt
1 cup coconut
2 cups carrots, grated
1 cup pecans, chopped

Frosting:
6 ounces cream cheese, softened
1 cup sifted powdered sugar
1/2 cup butter
1 teaspoon lemon juice
dash of salt

Sift sugar, flour, baking soda, and cinnamon. In a separate bowl mix eggs, crushed pineapple and juice, oil, vanilla, salt, coconut, carrots, and pecans. Add dry ingredients to the liquid mixture. Line 3 (8-inch) cake pans with waxed paper. Bake at 350 degrees for 35-40 minutes. Remove from oven and allow to cool on cooling rack for 30 minutes. To make frosting combine cream cheese, powdered sugar, butter, lemon juice, and salt. When cake is cool, frost layers and top but not sides.

Marcie's mother, Nancy Snyder, makes these beautiful cookies at Christmas—a perfect, colorful, healthy treat anytime. She dusts them with powdered sugar before she serves them.

Cranberry Oatmeal Cookies

1 cup butter, softened
1 1/2 cups sugar
2 eggs
1 teaspoon vanilla extract
2 cups all-purpose flour
1 teaspoon baking powder
1/2 teaspoon salt

1/4 teaspoon baking soda
2 cups quick-cooking oats
1 cup raisins (optional)
1 cup coarsely chopped fresh or frozen cranberries
1 tablespoon grated orange peel
1 (12-ounce) package vanilla chips

In a mixing bowl cream butter and sugar. Add eggs, one at a time, beating well after each addition. Beat in vanilla. Combine flour, baking powder, salt, and baking soda; add to the creamed mixture. Stir in oats, raisins, cranberries, and orange peel. Stir in vanilla chips. Drop by rounded teaspoonfuls 2-inches apart onto greased baking sheets. Bake at 375 degrees for 10-12 minutes or until the edges are lightly browned. Cool on wire racks. Makes 6 dozen.

Last but not least, who could leave out of a country-fresh recipe collection a how-to for Fresh Peach Homemade Ice Cream? It's as country as you can get. We just have to have this at least once a summer.

Fresh Peach Homemade Ice Cream

6 medium peaches (about 2 pounds), peeled and stoned, or 4 cups frozen unsweetened peach slices, thawed
1 cup sugar
3 cups heavy cream
1 cup milk
2 teaspoons vanilla extract

In a large bowl mash the peaches into a coarse puree. Stir in 1/4 cup of the sugar. Let stand for 1 hour. To the peaches add the cream, milk, remaining 3/4 cup sugar, and vanilla. Stir to blend. Refrigerate, covered, until the mixture is very cold, at least 3 hours or as long as 3 days. Stir the mixture to blend and pour into the canister of an ice-cream maker. Freeze according to the manufacturer's directions. Eat at once or transfer to a covered container and freeze up to 8 hours. Makes about 1 1/2 quarts of ice cream.

Index

A

Apple Bread Pudding 210

B

Baked Apple Pancakes with
 Caramel Sauce 142
Baked Apples 183
Baked Stuffed Onions 30
Blackberry Cobbler 124
Bonnie's Beet Pickles 147
Breaded Tomatoes 176
Broccoli and Cranberry Salad 157
Brown Sugar Apple Pie 204
Bursting Blueberry Pancakes 142
Butterbeans with Ham 68
Butternut Squash Soup 165

C

Cabbage Rolls 193
Cabbage Sausage Soup 169
Cabbage Sloppy Joes 192
Calico Beef Burgers 202
Caramel Apple Coffee Cake 141
Carrot "Pie" 177
Casey's Asian Chicken with
 Zucchini 202

Cheesy Potato Broccoli Soup 171
Chicken Corn Chowder 166
Chocolate Pecan Waffles 144
Chunky Chili 198
Cinnamon Apples 91
Copper Carrot Pennies 155
Corn and Tomato Salad 153
County Fair Chow-Chow 23
Cranberry Oatmeal
 Cookies 212
Creamed Turnip Greens 184
Crisp 'n Crunchy Salad 154
Crunchy Vegetable Salad 163
Cucumbers and Onions
 in Vinegar 111

D

Dawn's Bread Bowl 148
Deep-Dish Blueberry Pie 209

E

Easy Vegetable Soup 173
Eggplant Casserole 178

F

Fabulous Carrot Cake	211
Fresh Apple Cake	203
Fresh Garden Salsa	149
Fresh Peach Pudding	205
Fresh Peach Homemade Ice Cream	213
Fresh Peach Muffins	139
Fried Corn	186
Fried Cucumbers	174

G

Garden Slaw	154
Glazed Carrots	188
Grape Jelly	152
Green Beans Supreme	184
Green Gazpacho Soup	167
Guacamole	162

H

Harvest Softies	206
Hearty Country Beef Stew	172
Hominy Casserole	179
Honey-Peach Butter	150
Hot Bacon and Black-Eyed Pea Salad	159
Hot Cucumber Soup	165

Hot Sauce 182

I

Italian Vegetable Toss 158

J

K

L

M

Microwave Pumpkin Butter	152
Mixed Vegetable Casserole	179

N

O

Okra Creole 174
Overnight Coleslaw 156

P

Parslied Potatoes 182
Peach-Blueberry Pie 208
Peach Preserves 150
Pear Cake 206
Picante Sauce 181
Plum-Peach Crumble 44
Pork and Lima Skillet 75
Pork Chops with Apples 197
Potato Pancakes 138
Potato Soup 169
Pumpkin-Apricot Butter 151
Pumpkin-Pecan Pie 83

Q

Quick Peach Cobbler 103

R

Refrigerator Bread-and-Butter
   Pickles 146
Rocky Mountain Potato
   Chowder 168

S

Salsa 147
Savory Corn and Broccoli 187
Soft Tacos with Southwestern
   Vegetables 200
Southern-Style Greens 180
Southwest Mini Quiche 195
Southwestern-Style
   Succotash 188
Spiced Sugared Pecans 204
Stir-Fried Cabbage 177
Stuffed Green Peppers 190
Sunshine Gelatin Salad 160
Super Cereal Squares 207
Strawberry Layer Cake 49
Sweet Garlic Dills 149

T

Tangy Orange and Pecan
   Salad 161
Texas Pecan Pie Muffins 140

Thick and Chunky Tomato Spaghetti Sauce	196
Three Sisters Stew	59
Tomato Mary	164
Tomato Preserves	16
Tomato Relish	145
Tomato Sauce	181
Tuna Grape Salad	163
Turkey Cabbage Stew	170
Turnip and Onion Gratin	185

U

Upside-Down Pecan Apple Pie	210

V

Vegetable Quesadillas	191

W

White Bean Salad with Asparagus	158

X

Y

Z

Zesty Penne and Broccoli	199
Zucchini Au Gratin	189
Zucchini Bread	139
Zucchini Quiche	195
Zucchini and Tomato Galette	193
Zucchini Muffins	137
Zucchini Pizza Casserole	201

Other Family Books You May Enjoy

Way Back in the Country Garden by Kay Moore. If you enjoyed this book, share it with your friends and loved ones, who'll like it as much as you have.
_____ Copies at $14.95 = _____

Way Back in the Country by Kay Moore. Country recipes from six generations of an East Texas farm family, with colorful stories of the Three Red-Haired Miller Girls, encourage other families to preserve their own lore. Previous book to *Way Back in the Country Garden*.
_____ Copies at $12.95 = _____

When the Heart Soars Free by Kay Moore. Christian fiction set in a ski lodge, where a storybook romance faces severe challenges that force main characters to learn about faith and forgiveness.
_____ Copies at $12.95 _____

Gathering the Missing Pieces in an Adopted Life by Kay Moore. Adopted as a child, author shares her experiences of finding her birthfamily. A compilation of helps for adoptees, adoptive parents, and birthparents who are involved in this contemporary issue.
_____ Copies at $12.95 _____

Families of the Bible: How They Coped with Today's Problems by Louis Moore and Howard Hovde. Nothing new under the sun: biblical families struggled with today's same issues. Lessons learned from the Scriptures can help contemporary homes.
____Copies at $12.95 =_____

Add $4 postage and handling for first book, $1 for each additional book.
Shipping & Handling: _____
TX residents add 8.25% sales tax: _____
Total Enclosed
(check or money order) _____

Name _____
Address_____
City_____State_____Zip_____
Phone _____ Email _____
See address and other contact information on page 221.

To order more copies of
Way Back in the Country Garden

at $14.95 each plus shipping

Call us toll free:

1-800-747-0738

Mail the order form on page 219 to:

Hannibal Books
P.O. Box 461592
Garland, TX 75046

Visit our website:

www.hannibalbooks.com

FAX us toll free the order form on page 219
1-888-252-3022

Email us:
orders@hannibalbooks.com

LaVergne, TN USA
05 May 2010
181618LV00001B/3/P